119

JAIME SOMMERS

119

MY LIFE AS A
BISEXUAL CHRISTIAN

DARTON · LONGMAN + TODD

First published in 2016 by
Darton, Longman and Todd Ltd
1 Spencer Court
140–142 Wandsworth High Street
London SW18 4JJ

ISBN 978-0-232-53257-9

A catalogue record for this book is available from the
British Library.

Designed and typeset by Judy Linard
Printed and bound in Great Britain by Bell & Bain, Glasgow

From *Issues in Human Sexuality: A Statement by the House of Bishops* (1991)

5.8 The first is that of bisexuality. We recognise that there are those whose sexual orientation is ambiguous, and who can find themselves attracted to partners of either sex. Nevertheless it is clear that bisexual activity must always be wrong for this reason, if for no other, that it inevitably involves being unfaithful. The Church's guidance to bisexual Christians is that if they are capable of heterophile relationships and of satisfaction within them, they should follow the way of holiness in either celibacy or abstinence or heterosexual marriage. In the situation of the bisexual it can also be that counselling will help the person concerned to discover the truth of their personality and to achieve a degree of inner healing.

(119 words)

Dedicated to Ed, Carter, Kristen & DJ

with thanks to Celine and my previous employer,
who both gave me such valuable
support in writing this book

This is an autobiographical account of true events in my life. In the interests of authenticity, I've tried to tell my story exactly as it happened from my perspective. It isn't about attaching blame to specific individuals or organisations. Lord knows, I'm far from perfect myself. For that reason, I have changed the names of people and places where necessary to ensure the focus remains on the issue at hand, namely the difficulties faced by bisexual people of faith who want to live with integrity in a community that does not know what to do with them. This is not a book about the conduct of individuals, but an account of how the mental health of bisexual people is compromised by ignorance and denial of the phenomenon of dual attraction.

Contents

If you try me,
send me out
into the foggy night,
so that I cannot see
my way.
Even if I stumble,
this I beg, that I
may look and smile
serenely,
bearing witness
that you are with me
and I walk in peace.

Dom Hélder Câmara, *The Desert is Fertile*
(with thanks to Olivia)

Reproduced by kind permission of Orbis Books, New York

Foreword

by Jeremy Pemberton

I f what most Christians know about homosexuality could be written on the back of a postcard, what they know about bisexuality could definitely be written on the back of the stamp used to post it. Human difference is disturbing in all its forms, and, as we know all too well, sexual difference perturbs heteronormative Western Christianity greatly. Jaime Sommers' autobiography gives us one of the first narratives of how bisexuality and Christianity intersect, not simply at a theoretical level, but on the personal.

She writes rather like a Christian Caitlin Moran. There is an energy and directness in her approach to writing, as to life, that makes us sit up and take notice of her own struggles with embodiment. Her extroversion, her gift for making friends, her need for cuddles, her intelligence, her honesty, and her reluctance to play games, shout from the pages of this remarkable narrative. So, also, do the pressures that being bisexual brought upon her.

We are given a sparkling tour of her childhood in Wales, laced with copious, beguiling references to popular culture. Once into her adolescence, she manages to capture again and again the awkwardness of growing up, only this time with the added complication that she likes girls as well as boys. In a world before people talked about sex let alone LGBT matters, she communicates so well the shame and guilt that she osmotically acquired.

At the same time, despite her engagement with the evangelical and charismatic Christianity of the 80s and 90s, for which LGBT feelings were a matter for prayer, exorcism or healing, we still have the sense of a very lively character, caught between love of God and love of boys and girls, and wondering how she is to find her way.

Humanly speaking, the rock in the story is Ed, her husband. Clear from the start about his wife's bisexuality, Ed and Jaime embark on marriage and family. She had shown a gift for preaching and worship-leading from an early age, and when her youngest starts school she starts training as a Reader in the Church of England.

What happens to them next is the dramatic heart of the tale. It is a salutary story of love, betrayal, struggle and survival. It pits the failings and weaknesses of one person against the complexity, incompetence and cruelty of an institution. That what happens to Jaime and Ed is done in the name of God only makes it worse. As Jaime puts it so tellingly, 'There was an altar cloth of silence over the whole subject of same-sex attraction.'

At the end of it all Jaime says, 'Being LGBT is ontological; it's who you are at your core; it's not an acquired behaviour or a leisure pursuit.' *119* does the Christian community a signal service. For those who don't understand bisexuality, here, in narrative form, is the material to help you understand what is involved. For those who are starry-eyed about the way Churches manage discipline, here is a cautionary tale. Without doubt, they could have done it so much better. At a time when we are urged to listen to the stories of others, *119* is one unlike most. It deserves telling; it richly repays hearing.

Introduction

This is my story ...

A
pril 2015. I am at the Stonewall Workplace Conference in the QEII Centre in Westminster. I am a delegate representing my place of work, which is affiliated to the Stonewall Workplace Equality Index. It is the end of the afternoon and we begin to file in for the keynote speeches. Left of centre I see a priest who has impressed me earlier at a workshop on faith and sexuality, where he told his life story – a tale of pain, betrayal yet incredible courage in the face of brute ignorance and prejudice.

It has been a day of dignified testimonies and powerful stories. I envy these men and women their bravery and their freedom of speech. I take a seat next to my clerical friend. He looks less than impressed; it dawns on me that he has deliberately sat to one side to avoid interaction. But he gamely engages with me as I applaud his bravery. He tells me healing only comes through telling our stories. Until I find the courage to do so, my present will remain in painful bondage to my past.

There is power in individual stories, he continues. Until you speak your own truth, you will not have an authentic voice, and you will not taste freedom. I rally, what if you want to tell your story, but those close to you want you to keep quiet? Healing comes from telling your story, he repeats.

I want to be healed. I want others to be healed. I don't want anybody to go through the pain I've been through. So here is my story.

My name is Jaime. I am a cisgendered[1] mother of three who self-identifies as female, Christian and bisexual. I am married to a cisgendered male and have been for nearly twenty years. I live in a semi-rural village in England where I eke out an existence as an academic, a writer, a casual employee, a wife and a mother. As I progress through life, I shall undoubtedly shed some of these hats and acquire a few more. Some hats, however, will most likely stay put on my head. I just might wear them at a different angle.

Since the age of seven or eight, around the time I first started getting interested in popular music and television, I began to subconsciously note that I found both male and female people attractive – some more than others, as one might expect. The women were usually feisty – Deborah Harry of Blondie, Kate Jackson from *Charlie's Angels*. The men were an altogether more eclectic bunch – David Bowie, Evel Knievel and John Tracy from *Thunderbirds* (clearly a man with strings attached).

Around the same time, undoubtedly influenced by the Bible stories and parables recounted in assembly with such enthusiasm by my primary school headmaster, I began to develop a spiritual awareness. I had a sense of a presence above me and around me which I learnt to call God and Jesus respectively. I had been brought up in

[1]   I.e. my perceived gender mirrors the biological body in which I was born.

a non-church-attending family and this burgeoning faith was not encouraged in any shape or form. So church was not an option until I was old enough to make my own way to a large Pentecostal church in the city where I lived.

This was a psychosexual conundrum that was to define my life, and continues to do so until this day. I need to be emotionally and/or sexually intimate with both men and women to feel psychologically whole and I remain fascinated by the figure of Jesus Christ. I retain my faith in a loving creator God who sent his perfect Son to set us free; yet I need the love of the created and fallen to feel truly free.

Church dominated a quarter of a century of my life, until it became apparent that one could not live with any degree of authenticity between the binaries and find a place within the mainstream Christian faith community. There is no liturgical framework, no theology, no Christian ethic on how to live holistically as a bisexual or bi-intimate follower of Jesus Christ, whether sexually active or not. Church made me profoundly depressed. But life without the presence of Christ – as I know him[2] – would be infinitely worse.

One of my life goals is to find a Christian ethic or theology that enables bisexual people of faith to live with honesty and integrity, either inside or outside of the Church. An ambitious goal, some would say; others might be less gracious. *119* is the story so far of how I have attempted to live *my* life as a married bisexual lover of Christ. It's not an autobiography in the traditional sense of the word; this is not a blow-by-blow account of my life so far, but an attempt to shed light

[2]   I have no issues with male-gender pronouns for the Son of God, as I believe he came to earth in a biologically male body, probably for cultural reasons. That is not to say that I believe he is exclusively male in spirit.

on the experiences of bisexual people operating within a Christian framework. I hope in so doing to give hope to all the other men and women out there, living life between the tick boxes.

... this is my song

1

Ugly, Lovely Town

1971–1982

My name is Jaime Sommers and I was born in unremarkable circumstances to quiet bookish parents, in Bellshill, Lanarkshire, a former mining town some twenty miles outside of Glasgow. That's Jaime pronounced Jamie, by the way, as in *Magic Torch*. It was 1971, the year Britain turned decimal. I still have my first edition decimal coins knocking about in the attic somewhere. It was also the year Starbucks opened its first store in Pike Place, Seattle, and I have a souvenir mug from there, too, from a trip to the state of Washington in 1998.

I was born on 18 April, Sunday's child, 'fair and wise, good and gay', according to the traditional rhyme. Well, I have fair hair, albeit out of a bottle these days. It was the Sunday after Easter, known as 'Quasimodo Sunday' (for some obscure liturgical reason). A gay hunchback … the omens were not good! 'Hot Love' by T. Rex was number one in the charts, which perhaps offered a little more hope for the future. I believe Arsenal won the old First Division that year, too, which wasn't so good (I'm a Spurs fan). Samantha Cameron and David Tennant both share my birthdate – I hope they are suitably impressed.

I have one older brother, Simon, whom I've never

been particularly close to, but we don't *not* get on, if you know what I mean. Interestingly, since I've ceased attending church, we have become a great deal pallier and I can see us spending more time together once the kids have flown the nest. He's married to a Welsh girl, Angharad, and they have two children, one of each, just a little older than my own. I also have a brother-in-law and sister-in-law up in Geordie land. Hugo runs his own techy company and dabbles in local politics, while Ingrid is a part-time tree surgeon and GP.

As a family growing up, we were fairly self-contained (for self-contained, read antisocial!). From my mother I inherited honesty and a desire to please and treat others well, from my father, wordsmithery and wit. From both, I acquired a lack of height, green eyes and a complex combination of introversion and outspokenness. My tendency to push boundaries and sail too close to the wind I have inherited from neither of them, however. Their extreme risk-aversion has instilled in me a desire to live life to the full; growing up in such a quiet, routine-dominated environment has engendered in me a pathological hatred of scheduled phone calls, repeat vacations and all that is safe and predictable. My driver's licence is testimony to the latter!

It is symptomatic of just how quiet and puritanical my upbringing was, that the ultimate act of rebellion for me on owning our first house was to decorate the internal walls yellow and green. My parents have always painted every wall brilliant white, repeating the whole exercise (using the same decorator, of course) every few years for as long as I can remember. My husband Ed used to take great pleasure in commenting on the undercoat every time he visited, and enquiring in feigned innocence what colour they intended painting it! A psychologist would have a field day with my parents and their whiter than white external surfaces. However, white walls and minimalist décor appear to be very much back in vogue, so what do I know? It seems my parents were ahead of their time.

Ugly, Lovely Town

At the age of three, my father's job in the Civil Service moved us to South Wales and so my entire schooling took place in Dylan Thomas's 'ugly, lovely town' of Swansea. We actually had a choice between the two war-ravaged cities of Swansea and Coventry, so I could have emerged with a West Midlands accent instead! (Interestingly, my future husband spent his formative years in Coventry, so we could have been childhood sweethearts.) We started off renting a house in the Morriston area, as we waited for our house to be built. My earliest memories from childhood are of being reprimanded for playing in the gutter outside our house. (I liked filling my brother's toy tipper trucks with grey dirt.) What can I say, nothing has changed!

We then moved to our newly built bungalow in the summer of 1974, I think. A year or so later, I started primary school. My mother did not work at that time – not many mums did – but I do remember she got a Saturday job at Woolworths, that doyenne of the 70s high street. My father would take my brother and me to the local parade of shops on a Saturday morning, whilst she was at work. I remember having 25p pocket money to spend. That wouldn't even buy you a Freddo bar now, but at the time it afforded me a polystyrene glider or Fry's chocolate with money to spare, or I could cobble together two weeks' worth of pocket money and buy a chart single, which cost 49p!

The first 45 rpm I ever bought was 'Heart of Glass' by Blondie, though typically, I preferred the rather offbeat B-side 'Rifle Range'. I remember also getting a free copy of Plastic Bertrand's 'Sha-la-la-la-lee', oddly with my father's Braun shaver. Plastic Bertrand became a firm favourite and was indicative of an early predilection for the slightly anarchic and wild! My brother got 'Sultans of Swing' by Dire Straits from the same Braun promotion, and I think we fought over 'Maggie May'. (The first and only time I ever fought over a Rod Stewart recording, let it be said.)

My first album was 'Parallel Lines' by Blondie. I got

it for my eighth birthday in April 1979. I didn't have a Deborah Harry thing going on, though I admired her style (especially the orange jumpsuit from the *Union City Blue* video and the *Atomic* bin-bag look!). I was far more interested in the Blondie guys: Nigel Harrison (bass) with his curly mop head, and Jimmy Destri (keyboards) with his oriental eyes and cool 60s hair. Whilst I wasn't physically attracted to Clem Burke (drums), his wild thrashing percussion moves left an indelible imprint on me! (Check out the intro to 'Dreaming' for perhaps the best example.)

Growing up in the late 1970s was a time of austerity and boredom for most people. My parents' idea of a Sunday afternoon out was a trip to the local car showroom (usually Japanese and cheap) or some of the many parks on the west side of Swansea. At the former, we would skulk around bored whilst my father considered the dubious merits of a Datsun Sunny; at the latter, we would climb on the giant rocks (Singleton Park), visit the mynah bird and wrinkle our noses up at the permanent musky aroma of wet leaves and dog poo (Brynmill Park) or climb up the Rapunzel tower in Clyne Gardens (my favourite). Money was tight and we didn't own a telephone or a car until the late 1970s, unthinkable behaviour for families of today.

I whiled away the tedium at home by playing with my large collection of Playmobil. True to form, I was far more interested in the 'boy' characters, the builders and the policemen and the cowboys. The Playmobil ladies were predominantly blonde and Aryan with strange upturned tunics that closely resembled maternity dresses. Perhaps they were trying for the Nazi Cross of Honour, some thirty years on. The Playmobil *Frauen* seemed to exist in a permanent state of gestation, it seemed.

I did have Sindy dolls, but I was far more into my bionic woman toy, complete with bionic limbs and a pinging bionic ear. I had the second edition with the blue jumpsuit that came out in 1977. The doll was based on the character played by Lindsay Wagner in the Bionic Woman television series from 1976 to 1978, which was a spin-off from *The Six Million Dollar Man* starring Lee Majors. They'd femmed the doll up from the first edition, and she now had a red handbag containing a hair brush and cosmetics and matching red platform shoes! The first edition featured the bionic woman (minus handbag) in a tracksuit of the variety worn by the England national football team circa 1986, with the red and blue band across a white top. So my very favourite toy was a bi woman! Who says prophecy is dead?

I also loved watching *The New Adventures of Wonder Woman* in the late 1970s, starring Lynda Carter as DC Comics character, Diana Prince. I didn't have a Wonder Woman doll, though – I never really went for her glitzy post-telephone-box look. There did seem to be an awful lot of cavorting around in spangly bras and pants in the 1970s. I also had a soft spot for Gerry Anderson's *Thunderbirds* where, as I've said, I had a bit of a thing for John Tracy, the blonde one who lived a hermit existence at the International Rescue Space Station. I would have gladly kept him company, given half a chance, though I suspect the arrival of a self-propelled seven-year-old Nephilim in flares and a polyester polo neck at Thunderbird 5 might have frightened the living daylights out of JT!

I enjoyed primary school by and large, especially junior school. I can smell musty polished parquet flooring as I write! Our headmaster was a cheerful fellow called Mr Clothier and if he clothed me with anything, it was with a spiritual sense of the Divine and his Son watching over me. I was fascinated by the parables he told in class assemblies and whilst my parents were no longer churchgoers (they were Church of Scotland, which seemed to be some form of sectarian badge rather than a bona fide ecclesiastical allegiance), I somehow held onto to this sense of belonging to Jesus. I believed he was with me and I remember talking to God, though at that time I had no concept of prayer or the much-lauded 'personal relationship' with Jesus.

I recall telling my rather worried parents sometime around that period that I felt 'special' and different, but this definitely related to my faith and not my sexuality. My mother in particular was horrified at my delusions of grandeur and as I grew older, I gradually began to work out that church membership, or allegiance to a church once attended, did not necessarily equate to a living faith.

My earliest identity crisis did not centre on sexuality, however, but my Celtic heritage. Born in Lanarkshire to parents born and bred in Edinburgh saw me start school with a pronounced Scottish accent. Perhaps if my parents had been less shy and mixed a little more in the local community in Swansea, I might have had more of a hybrid accent (as I do now). But as it stood, I had the misfortune of attending a very parochial local primary school in a working-class area of Swansea. This led to much teasing by pupils and teachers alike on account of my accent and Scottish vernacular.

The worst day of the year for me was always 1 March, St David's Day in Wales. It is tradition in all primary schools in Wales to dress up in national costume on 1 March. The boys got off lightly, needing only to pin a leek (real or made from felt) to their school jumpers or perhaps a daffodil. (Some boys, it will not surprise you, took the size of their leeks very seriously, and it was not uncommon to see a small boy come into school bent double under the weight of an 18-inch leek pinned to his grey jumper – probably by his dad.) Most girls, however, were obliged to don a typical Welsh woman's costume of long black skirt, red or red and black checkered shawl, white high-necked blouse and a black stovepipe hat. (This was clearly a nod to tradition, as a typical outfit worn by Swansea girls does not typically cover so much flesh.)

There was no way, however, that my mother was

going to send me to school in what she perceived to be a statement of Welsh nationalism. There were no concessions to a 'When in Rome ...' philosophy, so throughout primary school, she would make me wear a kilt on St David's Day, with a token felt leek (smallest size available) pinned to my jumper! I was the school's first and only Celtic hybrid.

I was a bookish child, though how much of that was due to sheer boredom and late 1970s austerity I wouldn't like to say. Kids today, with their numerous electronic and audio-visual distractions and endless social outlets, don't know they're born, they really don't. However, I'm not ungrateful for those many hours spent alone with my nose in a book; it taught me to feel comfortable in my own company, plus it engendered in me a lifelong love of reading which has always stood me in good stead. Whilst my parents didn't go out of their way to socialise us, they did place a high value on the assimilation of knowledge. It was due to their diligence in this regard that I was often praised at school for my wide vocabulary and extensive general knowledge, attributes my husband and I have both been keen to engender in our own children.

I read books typical of children growing up in the late 1970s – Enid Blyton's *Famous Five*, *Secret Seven* and *Five Investigator* series and the *Mallory Towers* and *St Clare's* school series. I remember that for years I thought her name was 'Gnid Blyton', owing to her curly signature on the spine of the books.

I also read the Nancy Drew mysteries by Carolyn Keene, which featured super-sleuth Nancy and her two female sidekicks George Fayne (clearly a closet lesbian) and ultra-femme Bess Marvin. Nancy, I recall, had an oddly sexless relationship with Ned Nickerson. He clearly *did* keep them on, because there was no way he was getting anywhere with Nancy! I wonder to this day whether there was a bit of conservative evangelicalism going on in the Nancy Drew series, or just a bit of ill-disguised Sapphic love between Nancy and George. I also have my suspicions regarding Bess. She seemed to be over-compensating somewhat – perhaps to escape the evil clutches of George the predatory lesbian.

I also read the Hardy Boys books. Parker Stevenson played Frank Hardy in the late 1970s TV series, *The Hardy Boys/Nancy Drew Mysteries* – widely parodied as Hardy Drew and The Nancy Boys! I had a major crush on Parker. Pamela Sue Martin played Nancy (and went on to play Fallon the First in *Dynasty*). I also had a huge pash on Pamela Sue. It was only recently when I Googled the actors that I noticed a physical resemblance between the two (that Ted Stryker[1] blow-dry).

One of my favourite little hobbies at that time was editing these books for my own amusement. I once went the whole way through a *Mallory Towers* novel crossing out the 'i' in paints, so that Sheila borrowed Darryl's pants on a frequent basis – or did Darryl borrow Sheila's? I forget. What can I say? Life was not exactly swinging *chez nous*. Nancy Drew books always contained a few blank pages at the end. I would use these pages to add a love scene between Nancy and Ned, perhaps to atone for the lack of action within the novel. I think I shared Ned's obvious sexual frustration, even at the tender age of nine or ten! I don't believe I ever inserted a love scene between Nancy and George, which is interesting. I think possibly a bit of internal homophobia was going on there! Theirs was clearly the real romance going on between the lines.

A fortnight of the summer holidays was always spent at my grandparents' house in Edinburgh, where we reconnected with our Scottish roots. They lived in a three-bed semi in the Balgreen area of Edinburgh, near Saughtonhall Park and a stone's throw from Murrayfield. From their front window, you could see the big red-brick building that was Jenners Depository. (Jenners, for those

[1] Of *Airplane!* fame, *shirley* the best spoof ever!

who have not experienced the bourgeois splendours of Princes Street, is the Harrods of Edinburgh.) Across the road and round the corner was the local Scotmid supermarket, a rather Eastern European-style bleak local branch of the Co-op. The frequent clip-clopping of hooves could also be heard, as the milk was still delivered by horse and cart even in the late 70s. This would be punctuated by the sound of nearby trains whizzing along the line towards Edinburgh Haymarket and the permanent waft of malt from the North British Distillery, where my grandad worked. It's true to say, my grandfather permanently reeked of whisky.

I took particular delight in my uncle's vinyl collection whilst staying in Edinburgh. It was in Donald's strange pentagonal bedroom at my grandparents' house that I first discovered Bowie's *Changes One* – still a favourite album to this day – and basked in the sheer weirdness of *Hocus Pocus* by Dutch prog-rockers, Focus. I loved his chunky silver Hitachi turntable and the matching 70s-style headphones. Yes, Uncle Donnie, it was me who wrecked your needle!

Edinburgh itself is, from my perspective, by far the biggest jewel in the crown of British tourism. From the majestic castle on the hill to the regal stateliness of Princes Street, Scotland's capital is, for me, beyond comparison in the UK for beauty, culture and sheer awe-inspiring scenery. The National Gallery on the Mound is a particular favourite of mine and I was thrilled to see it feature so prominently in the 2013 blockbuster, *Sunshine on Leith*. The narrow side-streets and souvenir shops on the Royal Mile with their diverse array of tacky tartan tat are another big attraction for me, as well as staring down onto the numerous platforms at Waverley Station from North Bridge, or watching a cavalcade of claret and white buses trawl along Princes Street.

My paternal grandmother, also from Edinburgh originally, lived in a picturesque fishing village in West Wales called Solva, near St David's, and we would visit her once every few weeks, usually on a Sunday. In those days, the M4 stopped at Swansea, so it was a long winding drive along A Roads and B Roads, via Crosshands, Carmarthen and Haverfordwest to visit her. I had dreadful car sickness as a child, and I dreaded these two-hour trips, stuck behind tractors and dairy tankers. I remember once being so sick, I grabbed the nearest bag in the back seat of my father's car. It was a carrier bag containing my coveted collection of football-sticker books. They didn't survive. I was absolutely devastated – my Kevin Keegan sticker was wrecked, his perm ruined for ever.

If living as a Scot in South Wales posed my first identity crisis, my burgeoning awareness of confusing dual attraction was the next. I first became aware that I was different at around the age of seven or eight, as I recall. Welsh people are friendly and kind and Swansea folks are among the best. But in the late 1970s, early 80s, as my bisexuality began to emerge, it was, much like the rest of Britain, definitely not a safe place to share. So I didn't.

It started with having crushes on female actresses and sportswomen on TV. I noticed – as did my mother – that I always preferred the more aggressive tomboy women over the femmes. So it was Kate Jackson in *Charlie's Angels*, with Cheryl Ladd a distant second and Jaclyn Smith not even in the running! In tennis, it was Martina over Chrissie, and when it came to music, it was Suzi Quatro in her leather jumpsuit over Agnetha and Frida in sequined hot pants any day! Worryingly, however, I also had a bit of a thing for Gary Glitter, dressing up in what I called my 'Maggin Suit'. This consisted of a green sequined waistcoat, one of those slinky metallic polyester polo necks that were de rigueur in the 1970s and flares (a Maggin, for the uninitiated, is the creature that features in Gary's most famous hit, 'Do You Want to be a Maggin?').[2]

---

[2] He was actually singing 'Do you wanna be in my gang?' Probably not, on reflection.

Ugly, Lovely Town

The 1980s saw the emergence of the New Romantic music scene and beautiful androgynous men, influenced by Bowie and Bolan. I had a major crush on John Taylor of Duran Duran and David Sylvian of Japan. Their pouting painted faces adorned the walls of my tiny bedroom. In those days, you could buy poster magazines that opened up into a large glossy A2 of your favourite band or band member. I spent all my pocket money on these magazines between the ages of about ten and thirteen and these giant portrait shots of rouged men in Armani suits kept watch over me as I slept, wafting through my dreams with promises of yacht parties and dried Martinis.

Perhaps such bisexual crushes form a normal part of childhood. I vividly remember creating a super group on my bedroom carpet, with Sindy as Deborah Harry and my brother's Action Men as the Blondie guys. Sometimes I recreated Duran Duran, borrowing Sindy for Nick Rhodes. I would even 'bolster' their trousers to make them look more manly. However, whilst we all salivated over Duran and the Spands,[3] articulating any feelings for women was clearly off the agenda among my peers.

I was to find this out at junior school. As pre-teen hormones began to kick in, I would regularly develop crushes on girls. I longed to be noticed and cared for by older girls, a habit that has stayed with me. I always had boyfriends – boys on the whole liked me because I was feisty and good at football – but my feelings were never intense like they were for other girls. There was one particular girl called Kate who was the year below me at school. We developed an uneasy sort of friendship as the two tomboy loners in the girls' playground (how quaint that sounds now), kicking a football around the hard concrete yard in our cords and trainers. Kate was clearly allowed to express her masculinity a little more, because she had *real* boys' trainers, Gola or Adidas, in

[3] 1980s New Romantic band Spandau Ballet.

boy colours, where I had to settle for gender-neutral chainstore versions.

I think I was aware on a subconscious level that Kate was like me. She was like a mini version of her namesake, Kate Jackson, with a black pageboy and dark eyes (the negative film of my white blonde pageboy and pale green eyes). But she was painfully shy, bordering on the rude, and the friendship didn't last that long. It was more of a truce than a friendship, on reflection. Kate and I were like two outcasts, two alley cats maybe, enduring one another in the same territory without bonding to any extent.

One of the most painful episodes of my childhood was when my brother told my mother that I was following older girls in his class around at junior school and being a little affectionate towards them. My mother was furious with me and sent me to bed early. I learnt very early on that expressing feelings for other girls, however innocuous, was something to be ashamed of, something that was simply *wrong*. I internalised this shame from a young age, and consequently grew up with an enormous sense of guilt, which would see me take the blame for all manner of things for decades into the future. I suspect this was an experience common to many LGBT children of that era and I don't blame my parents for their reaction. It was a standard response born of widespread ignorance and social peer pressure. But it did mean that I felt I had to be beyond reproach in every way, academically, sartorially and socially, to gain their respect. It engendered in me a lifelong need to be perfect to gain approval from adults, and from women in particular, from schooldays right into adulthood. It wasn't enough to get 99 per cent in a maths test, it had to be 100 per cent. It wasn't enough to be quite popular, I had to be the cleverest, wittiest person in the room. I'd like to say I've grown out of such insecurity, but it wouldn't be entirely true.

2

Pogoing in the Spirit
1983–1989

Awkward crushes on girls and teachers would persist throughout my time at school, including secondary school and sixth-form college. Relationships with boys, which always stopped at snogging and a quick grope of the relevant zones (what the Americans term 'making out'), were a constant feature, too. It would be inaccurate to say that these served as a cover-up for my homosexual feelings: I genuinely found guys interesting and attractive and I liked the way they felt against me. I spent a large chunk of my childhood and teenage years snogging boys in the local park, and whilst I didn't perhaps find them as fascinating as some of my peers seemed to, they were certainly a big part of my life. There was no particular type: at ten or eleven, there was a slim, olive-skinned dark-eyed lad called Kevin, at fourteen, it was Jez, the plump, auburn-haired son of a policeman. At fifteen, there was green-eyed Jamie I met on a brass conference, and finally Rick, who was three or four years my senior and was later to die in a car accident. With all these lads, there was much furtive fumbling and hungry snog-fests, but never 'the whole shebang' – or should that be *he*bang?

I had a kind of mini breakdown when I was fifteen.

For me, fourteen/fifteen was definitely the nadir of my adolescence. I was brutally aware of my same-sex feelings and had awkward crush after awkward crush on girls and women alike. I do think it was exacerbated by being at an all-girls' school – hormones have to fixate on something, and in the absence of boys, mine homed in on the same sex. I had a particularly nice history teacher that year and I've always been a sucker for kind, older women who take an interest in me. But not only was she my history teacher, she was also straight, adult and unavailable, so I just suffered in silence. I know I went into my shell over my sexuality that year at school, as friends commented on me not joining in social activities (not that I have ever quite understood what is so fascinating about sitting on garden walls for hours on end gossiping about boys and clothes).

I just couldn't focus on my schoolwork and, added to that, the 1986 World Cup was on television and I've always been mad about soccer. (It was the 'hand of God' World Cup in Mexico, a classic.) History is one subject where, in my day, you just had to learn lots of facts parrot fashion – or at least you did at O level. There was no way I was going to remember which William Pitt passed which act in which order and all the rest of that deadly dull political history stuff we did for O level. I flunked my end-of-year history exam disastrously, getting 30 per cent. Because I was a straight-A student, especially in the Arts and Humanities, this was cause for massive concern.

I was taken to the acting head's office; she had previously been my history teacher and knew me well. She was very kind and asked me if there was anything going on at home to explain why I hadn't studied for the exam. I didn't reply, 'Yes, the World Cup', tempting though it was. And neither did I say a word about my sexuality. It was totally unmentionable in 1986. You just would not have talked about *that*, especially to a teacher at school. So I rather disingenuously blamed my poor parents, claiming that they placed a great deal of pressure on me to achieve and it had all got a bit much. She swallowed that and let me shed a few tears before sending me back to class. Most people who identify as LGBT will have perfected the art of lying fairly early on in their development.

Another embarrassing incident I can recall took place a year later, when I was undertaking a week of work experience at the offices of the local newspaper. Again, it involved an older woman who was kind and supportive of me. Ceryn was a features journalist and was responsible for overseeing my programme of shadowing that week. I think it was a measure of just how lonely and isolated I felt at home and at school, that I looked forward to seeing this complete stranger every day. Even though I loved accompanying the sports correspondent to football matches and hanging around with the other male journalists on the Sports Desk, what I really wanted was to spend a day with this friendly older woman, Ceryn. But it never happened and I felt quite teary about that. She actually noticed and asked if I was all right on the last day, which was mortifying. I muttered some excuse about things at home and made my escape. My poor parents were blamed for lots in my childhood years. But you need to understand, *nobody* talked about sexuality in the 1970s and 1980s, outside of lefty and academic circles. I mixed in neither, growing up in South Wales to parents who had both left school at sixteen.

As a means of avoiding the pain inside, I suppressed my emotions and threw myself into my schoolwork. There was no more flunking of tests or exams, and ten O levels, seven at A grade, bore witness to this in the summer of 1987. (On a side note, I'm pleased to have been included in the last year of O levels. I maintain that those who did traditional-style exams have a far more rigorous grounding in grammar and spelling than the GCSE generation, as one glance at my children's homework reveals!)

Perhaps the most disastrous 'straight' dalliance I had was with a small, effeminate lad called Paul Lyons in sixth form. At that time, I had a crush on the ITV weather woman and he had a giant cardboard cut-out of Freddie Mercury in his bedroom. In retrospect, it was comical.

Our first date was to see *Beaches* at the Odeon on Kingsway, Swansea. (What can I say, the signs were all there!) His mum picked us up, I think. Paul had *lashings* of aftershave on, chinos and a white shirt, with his dark hair gelled back. He had rough pimply, pockmarked skin, but the most gorgeous dark eyes. He wasn't a looker – there was a touch of the rodent about him – but he always smelled good and dressed well. I remember at that time he got a job at a newly opened gentlemen's outfitters in the Quadrant Shopping Centre in Swansea. He immediately offloaded about a grand's worth of suits, shirts and ties to his first customer, thereby winning 'employee of the month' in his first week there! He could charm the socks (and probably more) off people, and I found him strangely attractive, though with hindsight we were both probably using each other as a testing ground and cover-up for conflicting sexual emotions.

It gradually emerged, however, that Paul had a bit of a drinking habit, as most of us did at seventeen. However, he had the unfortunate habit of entirely changing personality and becoming a real loudmouth under the influence. Soon half of the sixth form knew that I had a crush on a certain weather woman (though can I just add, for the sake of preserving *some* dignity, it wasn't Wincey Willis!).

Then one night, when I had arranged to sleep over at his house (he lived seven or eight miles away from me), he got so drunk that he started throwing stuff around, including the contents of his own stomach, while yelling obscenities at me (his parents were on holiday at the time). I became quite frightened and rang my mother covertly, before deciding that standing outside in the street was probably the safest place to be. Paul followed me out and started bellowing drunkenly in the well-heeled cul-de-sac where he lived. I really was frightened of this small, effeminate, drunken boy. I think one of the neighbours forced him indoors at the time, and in record speed, it felt, my mother turned up in her little blue car to take me back to safety. She was a real hero that night.

Suffice to say, I finished with Paul. He was devastated once he sobered up and pleaded with me by letter and telephone to go back to him. He even sent me a 7-inch single through the post, 'Miss You Like Crazy' by Natalie Cole. Pure Camembert. My friends thought this gesture was hysterically funny. I did not.

Paul was not the only effeminate man 'playing straight' at tertiary college, and neither was I the only bi/lesbian masking my true self. I can think of at least three guys in my A-level classes who were definitely gay, one of whom had a makeshift girlfriend; the other two just didn't talk about it, though it was pretty obvious. There was also a Mormon girl in my English A-level class who clearly had a crush on her best friend, but understandably (from a religious perspective) wasn't going to broadcast her lesbian tendencies. I suspect her life wouldn't have been worth living, especially at that time, though I'm not sure the Mormon Church is much better these days.

Sixth form was a strange time for me, as I guess it is for many young people. Adulthood is forced upon you by virtue of your age, yet you still lack the life experience, logistical ability and financial wherewithal to grow into the shoes you wish to occupy, or at least try on for size. Added to that, for me, was the sheer inability to discuss anything of my internal struggles with my parents. It was a period where I almost totally retreated to my small bedroom, reading intently and writing poetry. I also threw myself into schoolwork, partly to mask the pain inside, but also because I was intent on getting fantastic A-level grades that would enable me to escape to university and away from Swansea. Most of the poems I wrote at that time were pretty dreadful. I was going to include some within this book, but they weren't quite the works of genius I'd remembered them to be! However, they do demonstrate not only my feelings for women, but also the intense pain and confusion these clandestine emotions were causing me.

I ached to be held and loved by a woman. In true Bonnie Tyler Swansea style, it was 'a heartache'. Some of the pain was due to the lack of approval and affection I felt from my own mother, who had always expressed disappointment in my lack of femininity and finesse. (Though I don't think many of my friends' parents would have behaved any differently, in all honesty.) However, I am reluctant to go down the parental absence/ parental blame route. My mother and my upbringing are responsible for many of my more positive traits, namely honesty, gratitude towards others, a strong work ethic, loyalty and reliability. My father has instilled in me a love of live music, wordplay and witty repartee, all of which are distinctly life-enhancing.

Without my parents' input, positive or negative, I would not be where I am today. As I get older, I realise that we're all just fragile constructs, doing our best to keep ourselves and our loved ones afloat in the stormy seas of life. Whilst there were many occasions where I felt my parents could have supported me more, there were probably just as many where I made it difficult for them to *feel the love*. There was some mutual exasperation going on, as per the passage from Ephesians 6. I now have a great relationship with my parents most of the time; undoubtedly we have all mellowed with age. There are still many aspects of my life that I feel unable to share with them, but that's a generational thing just as much as anything.

Christmas 1987 was a particularly difficult time for me, and perhaps the first time I experienced homophobia at a personal level. A group of us had gone to a bar in Swansea High Street at the end of term. Among this group was my best friend at that time, Jay, and her boyfriend Tony. The alcohol flowed and we were all a little tipsy. At one point, Tony decided to give me a big hug. He kissed me on the lips, I kissed him back – it must have been the alcohol speaking, as he had no redeeming features beyond a booze-fuelled willingness to buy everyone drinks. He then stuck his tongue in my mouth and engaged me in a full Frenchie. I pulled away after a moment, when through the drunken fug I realised Jay might not be best pleased with me.

That evening, I think it was 23 December, Jay rang me from the same bar in a furious drunken rant, accusing me of stealing her boyfriend and lots of other things. I was devastated. It had been a stupid drunken moment, and her friendship meant infinitely more to me than her lout of a boyfriend. That ruined Christmas; I was inconsolable. (I would, many years later, receive a drunken telephone apology from her and a newspaper clipping of her wedding photo – the first lesbian wedding in Swansea. My mother was horrified, and tried to stop my father sending me the photo.)

I returned to sixth-form college in January to find that Jay had told half of my year group that I was a lesbian. (I had told her in confidence a few weeks prior to Snog-gate that I thought I might be bi or gay.) As my college was some eight miles out of Swansea towards Llanelli, the natives were just that little bit more ignorant of the full spectrum of human sexuality. I was shunned by pretty much everyone for the rest of that year, until I found solace in two individuals who would come to represent just what was so difficult in my life – Roberta, who was a born-again Christian, fluent in the collected writings of Tony Campolo (a popular evangelical Christian writer and theologian from the US, who has recently adopted a more liberal stance on LGBT rights), and Mervyn, who played the violin, liked baking and had a strangely detached relationship with his girlfriend at that time.

It was through Roberta that I started attending church and Christian conferences. Whilst we are no longer in touch, I am forever indebted to her for inviting me to see Welsh folk singer Martyn Joseph at the Taliesin Theatre at Swansea University in 1988. For the past twenty-seven years of my life, I have seen Martyn in concert at least every other year, growing with him from monochrome evangelical Christianity to a more inclusive *Weltpolitik*.

Martyn Joseph, and specifically the *Ballads* album, was to become the soundtrack to my tearful prayers to God that Christmas. Alone in my room, I picked up the small claret Gideon's Bible that we had been given at secondary school and read the New Testament from start to finish. I became entranced by the figure of Jesus Christ, with his kindness, his cryptic words and – especially – his compassion for outcasts. Confused by my sexuality, wounded by the break-up of my friendship with Jay and exasperated by my parents, I wrote to the Gideons, pouring my heart out to these grey men, as I pictured them, about the immense sadness I felt inside.

They wrote back, which meant a great deal to me, and speaks volumes about the valuable witness the Gideons provided in schools, even if such visits are no longer in vogue in our multi-faith, politically sensitive society. I no longer have the letter, sadly, but I do remember that they told me not to worry and quoted 1 Corinthians 10:13:

> No temptation has seized you except what is common to man. And God is faithful; he will not let you be tempted beyond what you can bear. But when you are tempted, he will also provide a way out so that you can stand up under it.

It is only now, some twenty-eight years later, that I can see that God has been faithful and enabled me to stand up under the weight of my sexuality. At that time, I could not see that my temptation was common to humankind, because nobody talked about the subject, period. The pain and confusion often felt unbearable and I was struggling to hear God's answer to my prayers. Yet I held onto God, via his Son's hand. I guess that's faith, when you feel angry, cheated, inconsolable, yet somehow you still feel God there. It's only as I've grown older that I've begun to understand what Job was on about.

It was about this time that I started attending the Pentecostal temple in Swansea, where Roberta and I expressed mutual astonishment at both the monochromaticity of the sermons and the strange pogoing 'in the Spirit' that seemed to go on. The latter was performed on the stage by one of the church elders, wearing white tasselled footwear that were clearly golf shoes. We began to attend the temple for its comedic aspects rather than its spiritual content and soon people began to complain about our attitude. Time for a swift exit. What can I say … it was not gracious of us … but it *was* funny!

I do not remember homosexuality *ever* being mentioned in any church setting I went to. (I also attended a Baptist church in the Kingsway in Swansea for a time, once the temple was out of bounds.) It wasn't until university that I came to learn more about the Church's attitude to same-sex attraction and to delve deeper into the pit of despair that was being LGBT and Christian at that time.

Something else rather strange happened during the sixth-form years. In September 1988 – I know the date, because I was watching England win hockey gold at the Seoul Olympics – I was sent a poem anonymously in the post. It was stamped but not postmarked and my name and address were written in wonky caps. Inside was a rather tatty copy of Ted Hughes' poem 'The Wind', printed off on an old banda machine with smudgy purple ink. I have no idea to this day who sent it, or the significance behind it. The block capitals in the address sloped to the left, however, so it was probably a left-hander. Sinister indeed.

Perhaps it was an apocalyptic warning of impending doom, or simply a sign of stormy times ahead. Or perhaps the stones crying out in Hughes' poem was an oblique reference to Luke 19:40, where Christ says the stones will cry out in witness, even if the people won't. Perhaps, with hindsight, it was a call to activism? Who knows? But in any case, it seemed significant, and this poem has crossed my path again, as my daughter studies it for GCSE.

I know that my parents were very hurt and upset when I told them that I had to leave Swansea as all my bad memories were there. With hindsight, that was not a kind thing to say at all. But the pain of being unable to discuss – let alone express – my bisexuality with anyone had taken its toll. I could not see the situation changing if I remained in South Wales.

3

Thirty-Second Hugs & Toronto Blessings

1989–1995

The efforts I put into Operation Sanity paid off; I obtained three A levels in German, French and English Literature and an S level in German, easily obtaining the entry grades required for university. (I went to St Sebastian's University, having failed the Oxbridge exam rather spectacularly – a source of great relief both to myself and my parents.)

Getting my A levels was my ticket to freedom, since short of digging a tunnel under the Severn Bridge and hatching my own 'Great Escape', there was no other way I was going to flee the claustrophobia of my closeted life in Swansea.

Within an hour of unpacking my cases at my hall of residence at SSU (I was in Q Block, interestingly!), I had received visits from both the Chaplaincy rep and the Christian Union. Having been doused in an evangelical base coat during my forays into church life thus far, I elected to join the Christian Union. This opened up a whole new banal world of English Middle-Class Niceness to me, and I struggled throughout to fit in, being (by now) Welsh-accented, rather too forthright in my opinions and scornful of what I perceived to be a rather docile approach to the faith.

What I could not recognise in myself then was that in order to successfully suppress my sexuality, I needed my faith to be all-consuming, black and white and utterly devoid of nuance. This, if you like, was my day-faith, my breastplate of (self-) righteousness. I would pore over Scripture and Christian lifestyle books, desperately trying to 'pray away the gay' inside of me, self-flagellating with what I perceived to be the belt of truth. But by night, I would have my nose in some novel or biography of gay interest. The television dramatisation of Nigel Nicholson's *Portrait of a Marriage*, based on the unorthodox marriage of his bisexual mother to his gay father, was broadcast in the UK in 1990, and featured several scenes of sapphic love between the writers Vita Sackville-West and Violet Trefusis. I would watch this furtively on our black and white portable television in the kitchen at home in Swansea – it must have been broadcast in university vacation time – hastily flicking the channel over if my parents or brother walked in. (Such was life, growing up LGBT in the 1980s and 90s. Furtive channel-hopping was the norm.) Janet McTeer played Vita with sumptuous Oscar Wildesque arrogance and was truly superb. I have followed her career ever since.

Portrait of a Marriage introduced me to the grandiose and complex figure of Vita Sackville-West, and her loyalty to her long-suffering husband, politician Harold Nicholson. I immediately read the various biographies surrounding her love affairs with Violet Trefusis and Virginia Woolf, amongst others, and she became something of a muse for me. She still is, and the famous portrait of her, *Lady in a Red Hat*, hangs on the wall of our home – as some kind of reminder to be true to my bisexual self, I suppose.

I also read Radclyffe Hall's *Well of Loneliness* and *The Unlit Lamp* around this time. These truly were novels of despair that expressed the bleakness of existing as a gay woman in a patriarchal society. Whilst reading such books did not cause my heart to sing, they did at least remove some of my sense of isolation and confusion at the passions rampaging around inside of me. I was not the only one. Significant others had gone before me.

This inability to reconcile my faith and sexuality was not a battle I faced alone, either. As I became more involved in Christian life at university, I discovered many students struggling with the same torturous dilemma. One particularly amusing event saw a Christian Union friend at that time set me up on a blind Christian lunch date with a lesbian friend of hers, who was also a believer. To be honest, I was more traumatised at being handed a plate of baked beans than I was by the unexpected lunch date with Millie. Baked beans (as well as cucumber) have always made me gag. Anyway, I think the idea was that her lesbian friend and I would support each other in prayer, but, of course, some Fosters-fuelled cuddles in the Union Bar were far more appealing!

Millie and I did become spiritual friends in the end. I did not have sexual feelings for her, in truth. On the few occasions where we did get too close for comfort, I would be so consumed with guilt that, in the end, the guilt in itself acted as a deterrent. We enjoyed a close and fun-packed friendship, but it was always hard for Millie because she *knew* she was gay, whereas I was pretty much all over the place. I know that she was angry, hurt and downright dubious when I got engaged to Ed years later. Like many lesbians I have met, she had a hard time accepting that I could like men as well as women and did not share my desire to have children, which has always been non-negotiable for me. Millie was moving away from the Church, whereas I was, if anything, becoming more fervent in my faith.

There are very good reasons why Millie eventually left the Church, which is her story to tell, not mine. But suffice to say, some draconian conservative evangelical 'pastoring' from a local church did more to send her into the welcome arms of the nearest dyke than any gay propaganda ever could. Millie and I have since lost touch, though I did engineer a meeting a few years back. It was amazing to see her again, and she remains one of the key people in my life when I look back at all that has happened to me. As well as being incredibly funny, zany and kind-hearted, she is also a gifted songwriter, guitarist and photographer. However, though we just picked up where we left off conversationally, it was clearly awkward for her to have me knocking about, since she's now in a long-term relationship. So I'm not sure there'll be another encounter until we touch base in God's inclusive heaven. It's a shame; we shared so much together at university and had sooooo much fun, but hey, life goes on, people move on.

Another gay friend, Nigel, joined the Metropolitan Community Church (MCC) in London, which is LGBT affirming. He sent me their queer-friendly exegesis of David and Jonathan, but at that point I was too steeped in conservative evangelicalism to give these tracts the time of day. What a shame – it could have saved me decades of heartache. But then again, maybe I wouldn't have married and had three children, something I do not regret even for an instant.

In 1988, the now infamous Section 28 was passed by the Tory Government of that time under Margaret Thatcher. Section 28 made it illegal for local authorities to 'intentionally promote homosexuality or publish material with the intention of promoting homosexuality' or 'promote the teaching in any maintained school of the acceptability of homosexuality as a pretended family relationship'.[1] This created a climate of fear in society towards LGBT people, which was mirrored within the

[1] Source: https://en.wikipedia.org/wiki/Section_28.

evangelical church, fuelled undoubtedly as well by the growing HIV/AIDS crisis. Reparative or conversion therapies for LGBT Christians became the subject of Christian lifestyle books and conference workshops, where previously the subject was entirely out of bounds.

Several key books were published in the late 1980s, early 1990s period, which purported to heal the homosexual Christian. I have no desire to revisit these texts; in my view, they are profoundly damaging and I have long since binned my copies of such books. But the general position taken was one of nurture over nature: same-sex attraction is *not* inborn, but the result of dysfunctional parenting and poor role-modelling. A broken relationship with the same-sex parent was generally purported to be at the root of homosexual orientation and behaviour. However, these homosexual tendencies could be cured or significantly reduced by healing prayer and positive role-modelling, which allegedly could be found within the church family.

Much of the psychology was borrowed from Freud, Jung et al., but dressed up in God-speak for the conservative evangelical market. Any form of sexual activity outside of heterosexual marriage was sinful, therefore the Christian struggling with their sexuality must remain celibate. Homosexuality was a sign of fallen human nature and homosexual activity must be repented of, or hell surely awaited the individual in question. You can only begin to imagine the effect of such theology on vulnerable young adults, fighting desires and emotions inside of them that simply refused to go away – a battle that their straight counterparts had never had to fight. The 'ministries' in question were undoubtedly laden with good, if misguided, intentions. But in my view they placed impossible pressure on already defenceless individuals, pressure that was not exerted on those with heterosexual feelings, whether you believe in innate sexuality or not.

Leanne Payne's *The Broken Image: Restoring*

Personal Wholeness through Healing Prayer, published in 1981, was influential for a number of works that emerged in this late 1980s period, including Andrew Comiskey's *Pursuing Sexual Wholeness: How Jesus Heals the Homosexual* (1989). Briar Whitehead's *Craving for Love: Relationship Addiction, Homosexuality, and the God Who Heals* (1993) encapsulates in the title the position taken by the evangelical church on same-sex attraction. It was an illness, a form of addiction, like alcoholism, drug abuse or worse. They were cleverly written, combining plausible-sounding theories and counselling techniques, whilst appealing to the committed Christian's desire for holiness in the inmost parts. I would pore over these books, avidly studying the Bible verses quoted, praying in earnest, desperate to be 'cured' of my same-sex attraction. But nothing. Just increased loneliness and confusion.

Jeanette Howard's *Out of Egypt: Leaving Lesbianism Behind* (1991) was the one and only book for lesbians. I remember seeing Jeanette speak at the UK evangelical conference New Wine one year, when she spoke about the thirty-second hug (or was it twenty?). If I recall correctly, if a hug with a friend lasted longer than thirty seconds, then it was sexual, not platonic, and indicative of emotional dependency. What were we supposed to do? Carry a kitchen timer in our pocket to assess our friendships for amorous content? The thirty-second hug was a source of great mirth to me at the time; now it just makes me feel sad that such nonsense was ever allowed to see the light of day at a public event with vulnerable young people and adults present. What if that one hug from a friend, amorous or not, was what stopped a young person ending it all?

So not only was sexual expression outlawed for the homosexual Christian for ever, but also any form of meaningful affection. It wasn't exactly a message of hope, however much these authors and organisations tried to couch their words in terms of joyful release in the Spirit. We were promised 'freedom from bondage' by these books and their writers – I didn't have a 'bondage' problem! – but I never felt quite so shackled as when I read these gloomy guidelines for so-called Christian living. I didn't see the same stringent requirements being asked of my straight friends, who weren't doomed to a dry, sexless existence from here to eternity.

One incident in particular from my university days perhaps demonstrates this. I had a 'non-Christian' friend called Dan for a while. He was a bit of a tosser, to be honest, with his claim to fame being that he had lost the top of his finger in the Tiananmen Square massacre (he probably shut it in the car door). Don't ask me why – I was probably trying to prove something to myself – we ended up alone at his squalid student house one evening. We had a kiss and a cuddle on his bed, then he asked if I wanted to 'make love'. I have always had a bit of an issue with that phrase, to be honest. Perhaps it's because I don't feel romantic around men, just horny. In any case, it always sounds incredibly clichéd and mawkish to me. Maybe I would react differently if a woman said it to me. Or perhaps it was just the incongruity of Seedy Dan and his nine and a half fingers making the request. I often think 'processing lust' would be a more accurate description for the act itself, though that's not terribly romantic. 'Darling, let's process lust' doesn't quite have the same ring to it. I can't imagine Leona Lewis recording a clicky-finger love song with that in the chorus.

I suddenly came to my senses and made my excuses, feeling cheap and dirty for snogging this creep with his bullshit and stinky cigarette breath. What had I been thinking? I could have been pregnant with the seed of Seedy Dan if I'd let things take their natural course!

Amusingly, I went straight from Dan's bachelor hovel to my student church home group. It was one of those hot summer evenings where it suddenly pours with rain and the pavements smell of tar, I remember that. I arrived late with wet hair, looking dishevelled. I think my shirt was even undone a few buttons! What a hussy.

I remember telling the girls that I'd had a lucky escape from Seedy Dan and how ashamed I was at letting him snog me and 'cop a feel'. However, far from being shocked and righteously angry with me for my wanton behaviour, they all thought this was fantastic news, a sign from God that he was healing my broken sexuality via his secular messenger, Seedy Dan. These double standards amongst Christians infuriated me then, as they do now. It's fine to break the rules if it's a straight thing going on, but if you're LGBT, you need to be super holy and abstain from any form of physical contact. Why is the bar of holiness raised so much higher for LGBT people than straight people? Short of providing us with a large pole and asking us to vault six metres, they couldn't have set the bar any higher.

Another thing that got to me, and still does, is the privilege enjoyed by straight people. They don't have to justify their sexuality, it just *is*. They do not need to control who they fall in love with, or suppress their physical reactions. Yet they fully expect it of us, as if we have any more control over who we fall for than they do. They are *born* heterosexual, in accordance with natural law and God's plan, whilst we have apparently earned or acquired homosexuality/bisexuality. Why would *anyone* do that in such a climate?

One exponent of gay-conversion therapy in the UK at that time was a small, rather shy fellow called Jeremy Marks, whom I saw lead a workshop at New Wine with Jeanette Howard in the early 1990s. Jeremy's story is well known within LGBT church circles in the UK and I refer you to the Wiki article in the footnote below for further details.[2] But in a nutshell, Jeremy founded an ex-gay ministry in 1988 called Courage, which was affiliated to

[2] See https://en.wikipedia.org/wiki/Courage_UK.

the US reparative therapy outfit, Exodus International. However, by 2000, Jeremy realised that their gay–straight conversion rate was practically zero and that eminently more harm was being done to vulnerable individuals than good by attempting to straighten out homosexual identities. So he controversially changed tack, making Courage a LGBT affirming Christian ministry. As a result, Courage was thrown out of the Evangelical Alliance and with it Jeremy's livelihood.

Courage is a very apt name for an organisation run by Jeremy Marks. He is an amazingly courageous man. I cannot begin to imagine the crisis of conscience he faced in winding up Courage in its existing state as we hit the new millennium. I know that Jeremy's ministry has touched hundreds of people – men and women often in deep pits of despair because of their sexuality – and he is someone who has been there for me, too. Along with the Revd Sharon Ferguson of MCC North London, Jeremy was the voice of righteous anger that encouraged me to challenge the Church on its myopia over human sexuality when the proverbial shit hit the fan years later.

I will never forget one day that I met with Jeremy. It was 18 October 2012 and I was still in a pretty bad way from events I will describe later in this book. I had arranged to drive to Jeremy's office in Guildford for some much-needed spiritual direction. I think I cried most of the way up there and it was a pretty long drive. As I sat in a queue of traffic on the Farnham bypass, tears streaming down my face, I looked up at the green traffic sign. It said 'Shepherd and Flock Roundabout'. I think I knew at that moment that the Good Shepherd had my back!

I had a fruitful discussion with Jeremy and felt so much better on the way home that I drove through a thirty zone at forty-two miles an hour, thereby acquiring a £60 fine and three penalty points on my licence. I didn't bill Jeremy for the speeding ticket, tempting though it was!

So many ex-gay ministries have been forced to recant

– Courage, Exodus International – to name but a few, because it's just been found too difficult and too painful to change something so integral to your whole being. (Jeanette Howard, author of *Out of Egypt: Leaving Lesbianism Behind*, has now adopted a celibate stance, rather than claiming homosexuality can be healed.) And the effort of trying more often than not causes profound psychological issues for the individual for many years to come. Can that really be God's plan for our lives, that young men and women attempt suicide based on seven small lines in the Bible, irrespective of cultural context?

Jesus said that he came so that we might have life to the full (John 10:10). I see no fullness in living life spiritually tormented and physically isolated. That's not a full life; it's an empty shell of an existence. The Bible makes no such claims that the vast majority of us ordinary mortals should live without physical affection, whether that entails sexual intercourse, 'making out' or a thirty-second hug. And LGBT Christians are, for the most part, just ordinary people desiring the same basic human rights and privileges as their straight counterparts. Very few of us are called to a life of celibacy; why do so many in the evangelical Christian community have such rampantly different expectations of LGBT people?

The logical explanation for the failure of reparative therapy is quite obviously that sexuality is not changeable. And it's rarely for want of trying; I know I am not the only one to cry myself to sleep night after night, begging God to change my sexuality, immersing myself in Scripture and Christian lifestyle books in a vain attempt to render myself 100 per cent straight. But why would a God of love create a minority of individuals with a physiological predisposition towards same-sex intimacy that cannot be expressed, leading to psychological torture and profound loneliness? Why, when the majority can simply do what comes naturally without a second thought? It doesn't seem right to me. (Others will argue that it's the same for profoundly disabled people or those born with incurable conditions, but that equates homosexuality with physical impairment or disease, which is very dodgy terrain indeed medically, let alone ethically.)

So my time at St Sebastian's oscillated between bouts of extreme abstentious holiness, and furtive thirty-one-second hugs with both men and women. This made for confusion for all concerned, not least the Christian Union with their clean-scrubbed (heterosexual) upper-middle-class clientele. One incident in particular sums up the difficulties same-sex attraction posed for the Church/Christian Union at that time.

At that time, St Sebastian's University Christian Union had a devotional newsletter entitled *The Light*. Millie and I decided that it would be amusing to concoct an alternative magazine called *The Darkness* with LGBT-friendly articles. It was all rather anarchic, but we were lent credence by my now husband, Ed Sommers (very well spoken and ex-public school), writing an article for it. We ran off some cheap and cheerful A5 copies and distributed it to unsuspecting members of the CU.

Soon after, Millie and I were summoned by two female members of the CU exec (what can I say, it took itself very seriously!). Millie got good cop, I got bad cop, probably because I was the more aggressive and intellectual of the two of us, ergo the more threatening. In the end, bad cop, who shall remain nameless, was really quite nice to me. I introduced her to the music of Michelle Shocked as we discussed my rebellion, she introduced me to C. S. Lewis. She definitely got the better end of that deal. A lecture followed on how friends stood shoulder to shoulder, lovers face to face (lifted directly from *The Four Loves*, I believe). Direct interfacing with another woman was *not* appropriate. But bad cop was really quite all right in the end. In fact, I think I even gave her a full-frontal hug, though it probably only lasted a nanosecond, for fear I led her astray.

It was against the backdrop of this internal turmoil that I met, snogged and ditched my now husband, Edward Sommers, in 1991. We met through a mutual friend and there was an instant attraction. I have always had a bit of a soft spot for short, blonde men – and not only ones with strings attached! He was also a match for my razor-sharp mind and loved football, to boot. It was a match made in heaven – on one level.

Our first date was at a pub just outside of Aniton called *The Happy Boatswain*, where a large ginger cat that belonged to the landlord straddled our laps. (I had its head, Ed had its rear end!) I found from day one that Ed was easy to talk to. I knew my mother would like him. He was, as she put it once, 'genteel' – though I know quite another side to him!

I liked the way he dressed, in lambs-wool sweaters, jeans and leather shoes (never trainers) and I liked even more the way he felt against me. Cuddles with Ed have always been lovely, perhaps because he's just a little taller than me and well upholstered to boot (give me a bit of padding over skin and bone any day!).

We had some lovely snuggle-ups on his bed in his freezing cold student room, with its highly ineffective cling-film 'double glazing'. The cuddles were perhaps a necessity to stave off the cold, but lying there in each other's arms listening to New Order was very pleasant – though I would have preferred the more cheery Talk Talk.

However, after the Christmas break, I finished with him. The seismic aches for a woman had seized me over the festive break and I just felt it was unfair to put him through this. I explained to him that I liked women, too, and that I didn't know what I wanted and would just end up hurting him. He took it graciously, as he does everything, but I know it must have hurt, because it had felt so right for both of us before Christmas.

I studied German at St Sebastian's, so my third year of a four-year course would be spent in a German-speaking country. I elected to go to Austria, as I had undertaken a Youth with a Mission (YWAM) trip there the year before. I had fallen in love with the incredible snowy backdrops of Innsbruck and Salzburg and the palatial majesty of Vienna. But the city that stole my heart, where I would later become engaged to Ed, was Austria's second city, Graz. Lying on the eastern side of Austria in the province of Styria, Graz is a very green city with a famous clock tower overlooking the cobbled streets below.

I had an interview for my Language Assistant placement, where I was asked questions by a tall, bearded Austrian man at the British Council. I was subsequently given a placement in a small town between Graz and Vienna, not far from the Hungarian border, where it turned out that the tall bearded man was my GP! The placement threw me a little at first. I had asked to be placed in a large city, but this place had more cows than people!

Despite the acute culture shock, I threw myself into the local customs and soon made friends from both the Lutheran and Catholic churches, as well as building great relations with teachers at the schools I taught at and the older pupils. (I was 20 at the time, and my eldest pupils were just a couple of years younger.) As it was a fairly remote part of Austria, I had to speak German the whole time, so I returned from my placement year far more fluent than many of my cohort, though admittedly with a strong Styrian accent!

In the months before going to Austria, I knew I was faced with a choice. This was my real chance to start afresh, as an entirely new person in a different country. If I wanted to find a girlfriend, here was my opportunity. Or I could continue as I was, muddling through, throwing myself into church stuff and praying the gay stuff would dissipate in time.

I did some research, writing to *Hosi Wien*, which stood for *Homosexuelle Initiative Wien* (Vienna Homosexual Initiative). But it emerged that the promotion of homosexuality and public assemblies of LGBT people were illegal in Austria at that time, in accordance with Articles 221 and 222 of the law, the equivalent of Section 28 in the UK. Therefore, I would be placing myself in danger by consorting with this organisation, or so it felt. I was too scared to take the risk, so did not follow up the letter.

My year in Austria saw me travel to many of the newly opened up countries of Eastern Europe, where exhibiting any form of homosexual behaviour would certainly have got me beaten up or arrested. (I had already had one flirtation with the scary *Volkspolizei* in East Germany several years before, though that was on account of being tiddly in public, not sexually diverse) It was a very cultural year in many respects. As well as travelling to Hungary, the Czech Republic, Slovakia and Slovenia, I also went to the opera and ballet a lot in Graz and Vienna. I discovered that you could buy tickets in the gods for around six pounds if you turned up half an hour before. I managed to see *Swan Lake*, *Romeo and Juliet*, *The Magic Flute*, *Fledermaus* and *Madam Butterfly* amongst others via the lastminute. com option! There was also a coach trip to Tuscany with a friend, which took in San Gimignano, Montecatini, Chianti, Siena, Florence, Lucca, Viareggio and Pisa. However, my best moment was definitely roaring through the Hungarian countryside with my colleague Bernhard in his blue sports cabriolet, receiving cheers and waves from the impoverished locals. How very chavvy, but it *was* fun! The year in Austria otherwise proceeded much like any other year – a mixture of intense church activity combined with a gnawing ache to be held and noticed by women, left painfully unfulfilled.

I came close, only I didn't realise it at the time. A lovely elderly woman from the local Lutheran church, Frau Eggenberger, invited me to her farm in the Styrian backwaters. As was often the case in the countryside where I lived that year, there were geese everywhere.

(I can't begin to tell you how terrifying it used to be, making my way in the dark up the hill where I rented an apartment, with geese lurking around every twist and turn, ready to peck my ankles.)

When I got there, Frau Eggenberger told me that her niece, Liesl, would be joining us for lunch. I had met Liesl on a couple of occasions, once at a church gathering, and the second time at a reading of her poetry at the local wine bar/pizzeria. She was a 'mannish' woman, with close-cropped dark hair, very pale skin and a rather shapeless body. She wore a suit and grandad shirt and had a deep voice. Liesl was, to all intents and purposes, a bloke. Frau Werner, a woman from the Lutheran church who made me lunch every Wednesday, told me that she couldn't take to Liesl because 'sie sieht aus wie ein Bube' ('she looks like a lad').

Anyway, Liesl joined us and we had a convivial lunch, discussing her job as a departmental secretary at the University of Vienna, and looking at old black and white family snapshots. She was quite shy and very formal to talk to, and at least ten years older than me, but she seemed to like me and asked me lots of questions about university life in England. At some point in the afternoon, I dropped a mention of my boyfriend at home at that time into the conversation. I can't remember whether I did that on purpose or not, but I don't think I did. She left soon after and I never saw her again. I realised very soon after that it had probably been a set-up. I was not interested. I have never found butch women in the least attractive, and she was too serious for me, in any case. I need to laugh, it's oxygen to me! Plus, as I say, I was far too scared to pursue this line of enquiry in Austria that year. More worrying, though, Frau Eggenberger must have seen through my straight veneer.

I returned to SSU for my final year. This was to be the most difficult year of university for me, but not due to academic life, where I continued to thrive. In a nutshell,

I fell wildly in lust with a hilariously funny, blonde, blue-eyed sociology student called Sadie. We were part of an eclectic group of friends of all ethnicities and sexualities, mainly linguists and social science students (the usual clichés applied at St Sebastian's – English students were girly airheads; engineers were nerdy and uncultured; environmental scientists and geographers wore checked shirts and smelled of BO). Anyway, there were a few drunken snogs, but, as was becoming customary for me, guilt kicked in when it threatened to overspill into some serious action. In the end, Sadie got fed up of both my Christian chastity belt and split personality and it all ended very nastily and very publicly out in the street for all to hear. She was not the right girl for me, but as is my tendency to this very day, I put her on a pedestal and thought she was the best thing since a Breville toastie.

I was devastated and had something of a breakdown. It was around this time that I started flirting with a new Christian home group that had been formed by some old friends from the Christian Union. It was led by some of the trendier, charismatic members of the CU and met in a dilapidated old student house in a rundown area of town. I loved the sense of fun, as well as the deep love of Jesus, that resonated within this group and I started going regularly. It was led by a couple of guys, Marc and Andy, who are now prominent figures in a leading evangelical church movement. However, without being a friend of Millie's, I would never have found out about it.

I had got fed up with Marc constantly asking me how Millie was whenever I bumped into him. It was well known that Millie had left the church and moved in with a woman and it was a subject of much consternation and genuine concern amongst our peers. A few daring members of the CU rang her and one kamikaze soul even paid a visit to her new digs. (Oh, to have been a fly on the wall at that rendezvous!) Anyway, one morning I just turned my head to Marc on our stroll to uni and said: 'Why don't you ask how *I* am for once?'

Perhaps, with the benefit of adult hindsight, that was what Marc was trying to do by engaging me in the only real subject we had in common outside of Christianity. In any case, my annoyance led to the invite to the home group, which was to become an important part of my life for the next four years.

I'm proud to say I was one of the initial batch of disciples in that home group, a group that went on to achieve much greater things. The combination of professional-level worship, both acoustic and rock, coupled with Spirit-filled prayers and prophecies and absolutely *no* long boring sermon, made for an attractive mix for young adults at the more hip end of the spectrum of believers. It was very much spiritual dessert without the main course, but that's kind of what I wanted at that point in time. There was way too much hard-hitting 'meat' in the churches at the time, meat that was overcooked and dry to the palate.

We grew in number and applied to be affiliated to the charismatic evangelical free church known as the Fellowship of Believers (or FOB), which had its origins in the USA. This duly happened and meant that an established church oversaw us, which opened up a whole new world to us of church events and conferences around the country – and in the USA, if you were blessed enough to be on the leadership team. The music was on trend, the message exciting. However, homosexuality was still seen as a sin, a form of sexual addiction that needed 'prayer ministry' or 'inner healing'. This was universal in the free evangelical church at that time, and still is within many conservative churches. But at least they were acknowledging the existence of LGBT people and discussing the subject, which was more than the mainstream denominations were at that time.

One particular event that stood out for me was a Soul Survivor youth conference in the early 1990s. I had blagged myself a place there on the cheap by joining the Detached Youth Team. This involved speaking to errant teenagers who were not attending the workshops or worship sessions, to find out if they were okay and if they needed help with anything. It was not a popular ministry to be part of, as it meant you missed the main worship sessions and most of the teaching workshops, so it was usually possible to get a subsidised pass to the event if you agreed to be on this team.

The only problem was, I myself was one of those detached youth. I had nothing to offer these lonely misfits, because I was one myself, beneath the bravado and Christian rhetoric. A slight, blonde girl of about fifteen whom I spoke to told me she thought she might be gay. That was particularly hard, because I found myself telling her what I *ought* to tell her, namely that she wasn't stuck with these feelings for ever, and that God could heal her. But at the same time, I felt a longing just to hug her and give her comfort, because she was clearly suffering, and I think I knew deep down that nothing would really change for her. Or for me.

It was at one of these events that I first saw Steve Chalke in the flesh, which wasn't an altogether unpleasant sensation at that time. He was delivering the talk at either a Soul Survivor or New Wine conference in the early 1990s, I forget which. He absolutely lambasted the young girls there from the pulpit for walking around in skimpy clothes at a Christian event, and expecting young men not to struggle with temptation. I actually applauded him, because the double standards thing was a constant source of irritation for me. Why did LGBT Christians have to live monastic lives, while straight ones could trollop around flaunting their sexuality to all and sundry, acting no differently from non-believers?

These conferences often featured healing workshops led by Mary Pytches, author of *A Child No More: Growing into Christian Maturity* (1991) and *Yesterday's Child:*

Healing Present Problems by Understanding the Past (1996). Again, the titles of these books should tell you what her position was on homosexuality. Whilst these books did not focus exclusively on the gay thing, and were generally more about overcoming insecurity and negative behaviour patterns, I certainly remember homosexuality being portrayed as sinful and a result of insufficient bonding with the right parent at the appropriate time in childhood.

I enjoyed Mary's workshops a great deal, and I loved listening to her teaching tapes. I found her wise and funny, with a genuine heart for helping people move on and grow in faith and maturity. She was a clever and kindly woman, as was her sidekick and co-author Prue Bedwell. But looking back, it didn't deal with the lived experience of actual individuals struggling with same-sex attraction or gender fluidity, who found that all the prayer ministry in the world wouldn't plug the gaping hole inside.

I often wonder how the ex-gay writers from that era who haven't recanted feel in 2016, now that same-sex marriage has been legalised in the UK and public opinion has generally become accepting of homosexuality. It seems to me that the established Church, the Church of England, is bordering on appearing disreputable in the eyes of the general public for refusing to grant the same rights to gay people in love as to straight couples. I firmly believe that homophobia will be classified alongside racism, sexism and anti-semitism as one of humanity's great own goals. I know which side of the tracks I want to be on, when the horror documentaries start appearing on Channel 5. As one church leader over the pond commented, better to be taken to task at the pearly gates for being too loving and accepting, than too judgemental. History will show the rejection of LGBT people in our churches to be a heinous sin and a grave injustice. I have absolutely no doubt about that.

After I finished my first degree in 1993, gaining First

Class Honours in German, I really didn't know what to do with myself. I have never had a career path mapped out; all I have ever wanted to do is write books and be a public speaker. As I had a language degree and MFL teachers were in short supply, I was offered a funded place on a postgraduate teacher training course at SSU.

So I spent a year doing teaching practice at some rough-and-tumble local secondary schools. I enjoyed the teaching aspect and got on famously with the kids, as I, too, had gone to a dilapidated, inner-city comprehensive so could identify with them totally. However, I hated the demands it made on my spare time. I was trying to write my first full-length novel and lesson prep just got in the way. I decided it wasn't for me, which didn't go down too well, since I had received Government funding for it. I then got a place on a masters course in European Studies in 1994, again funded by SSU, this time because I was a graduate with First Class Honours. I didn't enjoy this much either; too much impenetrable French philosophy (in French) for my liking, but it did enable me to carry on my involvement in FOB. (Foucault and Derrida have come back to haunt me in my doctoral studies, so that will teach me for not paying more attention!)

These were exciting times at FOB and in the evangelical church in general. A phenomenon known as the Toronto Blessing had come over from a church called Toronto Airport Vineyard in Canada. It was allegedly a manifestation of the Holy Spirit, which caused those filled with the Spirit to behave in all manner of crazy ways. Some people laughed, some people fell to the floor, some people engaged in weird spasmodic dance moves, whilst others barked like dogs. Yes, really.

I remember having hands laid on me by the church leaders when I was selected for leadership of a home group. I started laughing uncontrollably, which had a 'laughing policeman' effect on the rest of the congregation. For a while, as soon as anyone prayed for me, I would begin to sway, often falling backwards into the waiting arms of the 'ministry team'. It all sounds so ridiculous and pompous now I'm in Civvie Street and part of the left-wing *Guardian*-reading establishment, but it felt very real and right at the time.

I started to doubt the integrity of all this when it became clear that the same couple of women would fall over at every meeting. It felt odd that the Holy Spirit would home in on these two individuals each time. It became obvious they needed the attention, whether this was intentional attention-seeking or not. There was an in-church adage at that time: it's not how you are when you fall down, it's how you are when you get back up. Maturity tells me this is a somewhat hackneyed piece of received wisdom that is true of most adverse circumstances in life, but at the time it felt quite profound. If God was truly changing these women, why did they need to keep seeking prayer ministry and affirmation from others? Maybe that was harsh of me, but I've never been able to stand attention-seeking in any form, especially in women, probably because nobody paid much attention to my emotional needs when I was growing up.

Now I think the hysterical fits of laughter that befell me was probably my subconscious giggling in mirth at the whole situation. Whatever the Toronto Blessing was all about, it seemed to alienate individuals and churches from each other, rather than lead to a revival of any lasting merit. It encouraged you to focus in on yourself and what was going on with you spiritually, rather than looking out for others in a practical, grounded way. In that sense, it wasn't a million miles from consulting your horoscope or other self-indulgent, narcissistic habits. This self-absorption at the expense of caring practically for others was endemic within the evangelical church at that time, both sides of the pond, or so at least it seemed to me. And I was perhaps more self-absorbed than many, owing to my inner conflict.

I went through a phase of watching the American preacher Joyce Meyer on the God channel around this time. It became addictive, watching this grandma in shoulder pads from St Louis, Missouri, march around on stage belting out a combination of homespun sagacity and Scripture. Looking back now, I was just so desperate to make the pieces all click into place, I'd absorb anything that felt vaguely like it might bring wholeness. I subscribed to her newsletter and had some teaching tapes. Slowly something began to bother me about Joyce Meyer's ministry though, beyond the private jet rumours. I couldn't quite put my finger on it at first, but then I realised: it was all about the individual. How can I improve *my* walk with God? How can *I* be more effective for God? Me Me Me. The great irony of it all was that she had become famous for her robot walk across the stage, in which she would castigate self-obsessed, insecure church members by chanting 'What about me? What about me? What about me?' in a robot voice. But the message of the Gospel is to sacrifice our ego in worship of Christ and in practical service of others. I actually took the time to write to Joyce Meyer – or her admin team at least – to explain why I was cancelling my monthly subscription. I did get a polite letter back, but it was generic and did not address my concerns. I was not surprised. The Prosperity Gospel is all about personal victory, not about criticism or failure.

The year 1994 was also a significant one as it was when the first ever lesbian kiss was broadcast on British television – when Beth Jordache (played by Anna Friel) in Scouse soap *Brookside* snogged her best friend, Margaret, following an altercation with a Christmas tree. It was January time, and I was at home from university. I remember asking my mum, what would you have done if one of us had turned out gay? My mother pursed her lips as she is prone to doing and made it abundantly clear in clipped Edinburgh tones that a lesbian offspring would not be welcome at the table. I don't expect for one minute that her reaction was untypical of anyone her age at that point in time, but it still shocked me. It underlined my growing conviction that it was just too hard to have gay feelings, and better just to throw myself into church and study and pretend they weren't there. I did like guys, and they clearly liked me, and I preferred their company on the whole. It shouldn't be too difficult, if I put my mind to it. After all, it wasn't as if I was totally gay or anything.

It was around this time that Ed came back into my life. At the time I was sharing a house with the same mutual friend in Aniton who had introduced us four years previously. Unknown to me, she had invited him down for the weekend, then promptly disappeared off to the cinema with a friend.

So when the doorbell rang at around 7 o'clock that Friday evening, I opened the door to a smiling Ed Sommers. What followed is a source of amusement and embarrassment to me in equal measure. What can I say? There followed a hug of beyond thirty seconds, complete with a long kiss with tongues! I don't think we even uttered a word to one another before the embrace. Let's just say, the old feelings were still there. He did look particularly fetching in a black polo shirt and jeans. Talk about a set-up!

Whilst there were doubts at times, I think I knew from that moment on the doorstep onwards that we were right together. The old easy conversation took off where it left off, and I also discovered that Ed was attending an FOB church back home in London. We started dating again, but this time it was serious.

4

Officially Straight: The Housewife Years

1995–2009

Ed and I were engaged below the *Uhrturm* (Clock Tower) overlooking the city of Graz, Austria, one sunny day in October 1995. We were both twenty-four-years old. It was planned to happen that holiday, although I left it to him to choose his moment (kind of). Okay, so I'm a bit of a control freak!

Back home, Ed's mother and grandmother were less enamoured. I was not the girly, public-schooled future daughter-in-law they had had in mind. To their eyes, I was pursuing a *vacation* rather than a *vocation*, having decided teaching was definitely not for me. However, I gradually won them over when they could see how well suited Ed and I were at most levels. And, I have to say, Ed's mother was far from the ideal mother-in-law I had envisaged. I had hoped for a cuddly, empathic, youngish, laugh-out-loud mother-in-law, someone who would be a close friend and companion as well as family. It was not to be, though I must concede to finding her highly amusing the more I got to know her! It would be fair to say she preferred shrubs to people – or at least, that's how it felt at times. That said, we ended up developing a great relationship and I cried my eyes out when she passed away last year. She was very generous to me and I never quite realised how much she meant to me until she wasn't there any more.

The next year was a whirlwind of planning the wedding and buying our first house. Ed had found a job forty minutes' drive away, which enabled him to share a house with some lads from FOB and commute back and forth to the area where I was renting at that time. By this time, I had finished and passed my masters degree. I had been offered a PhD place, but the subject matter didn't interest me, and to be honest, I had had enough of studying at that point in time. I continued with some temping work I had picked up, as it was flexible and allowed me to do wedding stuff and carry on church activities.

On the whole, my friends were positive about my engagement to Ed. A few close friends, however, were dubious that the marriage would be able to survive the issue of my bisexuality. I certainly had my own doubts – never that Ed was not the right man for me, just that the best man on the planet could not take away the ache inside.

I wouldn't say I buried my head in the sand about the inevitable complexities posed by my dual sexuality, more that I played a percentage game. Most of the time, things were fine. When it hurt, it really hurt, but who had a perfect life anyway?

It was time to get away from the university environment and embark on adult life. We purchased a two-bedroom cottage, still in Aniton but in a non-student neighbourhood, although we didn't cohabit prior to our wedding for faith reasons. (We both agree, on reflection, now that we have a less legalistic, more embodied understanding of the Christian faith, that holding back sexually until we were married was not necessarily helpful for either of us.) The preparations for the wedding were stressful. My parents were not happy that I wasn't getting married in Swansea. Whilst I understood that my mother wanted all of her friends to see me married from home, it just wasn't practical. Ed's elderly grandmother would have been too frail to have made the journey from London to Swansea; it was inconceivable for Ed that we married without her present. In addition, Swansea had never felt like home, perhaps because I was not Welsh to start off with, while Aniton very much did.

Given the distance between Swansea and Aniton, my parents felt unable to be involved in the planning of the wedding, so Ed and I had to do it all ourselves. Our friends from FOB helped us out, but it remained stressful. I stopped eating, as I tend to do when I'm stressed, and went right down to seven and a half stone. This meant that Helena, a colleague from work who was making my wedding dress, had to keep taking it in (even so, I spent a large chunk of my wedding day hoiking up my dress to keep myself decent!). I remember my housemate at that time, Clara, force-feeding me doorstep ham sandwiches so that I didn't waste away entirely before the big day.

I confess, I was very nervous leading up to the wedding, which was to be held at a large Anglican church in the parish where I was still renting a house with two teachers. The arrangements were in hand, with the help of my FOB friends and housemate, but as it drew nearer, I started panicking about our wedding night and marriage in general. Although I had 'made out' with both men and women – though primarily men – throughout my teenage years and early twenties, I had never quite gone all the way. What would it be like? Would I freak out?

Ed was panicking on our wedding day as well, which took place on a sunny Saturday in September 1996. His panic set in at around 2.15 in the afternoon, when I still hadn't turned up for our date at the altar, which was scheduled for 2 o'clock. The truth of the matter was, our wedding car, which had to travel a couple of miles from the hotel my family were staying at to the church, had got stuck in Saturday afternoon football traffic. These were the days before everyone treated mobile phones as extended bodily parts, so there was no question of warning Ed. (And can you imagine the panic that would have ensued had his mobile gone off while he was waiting nervously in the front pew?)

I finally walked down the aisle at 2.30 pm on my proud father's arm. Ed looked mightily relieved. I guess there was a fear I would have bottled it in the circumstances. My chin was wobbling all the way down the long walk to the altar. I was holding back tears, a combination of nerves, anxiety at what I was signing up for and sheer self-consciousness at so many people turning to stare at me in a dress! But as soon as I stood next to Ed, the nerves dissipated. The service went well, with fantastic contemporary worship from the FOB band. A friend of Ed's from his FOB days in West London delivered the sermon and my housemate, Clara, read a prayer.

The reception went well and our speeches went down like a house on fire. There was some opposition from the older generation about me making a speech, but there was no way I was going to let Ed have the final word. My father, king of bad puns, probably stole the show, though, especially when he produced a handwritten letter from Barry Venison, the much-travelled mulleted footballer from the North East, whom I'd embarrassingly had a bit of a crush on during his Sunderland days! As the letter was written on a notecard featuring Constable's painting of Salisbury Cathedral, I am guessing my parents sent Barry a pre-franked card to fill in. Anyway, Barry wished me well, and hoped that my taste in men had improved!

How was my wedding night? Well, what goes on in the bedroom stays in the bedroom. We stayed the first few nights at a local hotel, then enjoyed a honeymoon in the Gambia, on the west coast of Africa, where the cockroaches in the en suite were by far the scariest thing in the bedroom!

Married life was generally great. Many of our friends had recently got married, too, so there were many dinner parties and social gatherings in the area where we lived. The summers of 1996 and 1997 were our 'Four Weddings' summers – the funerals would come sooner than expected, though, which I will touch on later in this chapter. At this time, I was working as a translator for a local firm in Aniton. I was finally using my degree, but the work was dry and antisocial. My boss was a charismatic, fundamentalist Christian. He was a lovely, generous man, but he micromanaged me, which I found quite overbearing, though understandable I suppose when you're running your own business. I found this, coupled with his 'in your face' evangelical faith, a bit too much to take. So I left after two years and immediately got an admin post back at St Sebastian's, where I worked for two years prior to going on maternity leave in the summer of 1999.

By this stage, I was beginning to become disillusioned with the whole charismatic evangelical church thing. Despite throwing myself into FOB and the charismatic movement, the very real, organic, carnal pain inside persisted. It's hard to explain, because I was not unhappy. It was wonderful being married to Ed; we were – still are – ridiculously well suited. But there was this other part of me that he just couldn't reach. I had a brief 'romantic friendship' with an Irish girl from church, but it didn't come to anything, which was good because I felt guilty as hell about having these feelings for her. She wasn't even worth it and in total denial about her sexuality in any case. Every time something like that happened, I would just feel so bad inside that I would throw myself even more fervently into church stuff. It was mentally exhausting, this switching between modes the whole time.

One event in particular precipitated our decision to leave FOB and join the local C of E. Hot on the heels of the Toronto Blessing of 1994 came the Brownsville Revival, also known as the Pensacola Outpouring, in the summer of 1995. If Toronto was about being positively blessed and empowered by the Holy Spirit, Pensacola (as we knew it) was more about conviction and judgement. The revival had started in an Assemblies of God church in Pensacola, Florida, and was a Spirit-inspired call to repentance and holiness. Whilst there were, in common with Toronto, features of religious ecstasy in the Pensacola Outpouring, it was the conviction of sin that characterised this particular revival.

News of events in Pensacola filtered through to the FOB church locally, and soon our leaders had gone out to Florida to witness the phenomenon for themselves. They came back – it felt – full of hell, fire and brimstone, preaching a strong message of repentance to all of us. For a while it seemed like every church service we attended, the bar of personal holiness was raised higher and higher, until it got to the point that you felt you might as well not get out of bed in the morning, to save yourself from sinning. But then you'd be strung up for sloth. Ed in particular got very put off by the negativity, and began to long for his home FOB in London, which was altogether less reactive to the latest fads, having a more mature, professional congregation. It was a fairly pointless longing, given the distance between London and our home in Aniton.

The end of our time at FOB came when a Pensacola Revival event was held at the parish church near our house, which was soon to become our 'local', though we didn't know that at the time. A number of charismatic churches were invited to share in a worship and prophecy service, and some congregants from the parish church turned up, too. The church was packed. It started off okay, with fantastic musical worship, but from there it all got out of hand. Soon all manner of weird and wonderful prophecies, as well as noises, were emanating from the front. Ed and I were looking at each other, shaking our heads. In the end, we just walked out in disgust. I remember on the way out telling our pastor that the whole thing was out of control. He agreed. Because it was.

Another thing that fuelled my personal desire to leave FOB was the lack of opportunities for using my gifts. I have always had a talent for public speaking, winning several competitions in my school days and, of course, I was a qualified teacher. In FOB, much like the rest of the charismatic church, a rule of male headship existed at that time. That meant that women could not exercise authority over a man, therefore couldn't teach men in a church setting. It was fine for them to teach other women or children in other settings, but not preach the sermon at church on a Sunday. At FOB, all home groups had a male and female leader, but the female deferred to the male. Women could teach other women, look after children, bake quiche or sing/play in the worship band (so long as they were pretty, pure in spirit and not prone to smoking fags). This was standard across the board at free churches. But it was pretty frustrating if, like me, you did not excel in all-female company, quiche-making, musical worship or looking pretty.

In 1997, we joined the local C of E church, All Saints. It was not Ed's desire, but we wanted to remain in the Church per se, and it was the most expedient option, especially since my old housemate, Clara, and her now husband worshipped there. I clearly remember the first time we went to All Saints following our decision to leave FOB: it was Sunday 31 August 1997, the day Princess Diana died.

Earlier that morning, Ed had woken me up, telling me something cataclysmic had happened. It takes a lot, and I mean a lot, to get me out of bed in the morning (usually a large mug of strong filter coffee does the trick), but I could see in his face that something major had happened. Like many people, we spent most of the morning in our pyjamas, silently absorbing the gruesome incoming news reports of how Diana was killed in the tunnel in Paris.

Officially Straight: The Housewife Years

Three subjects dominated the news in the 1980s when we were growing up: the conflict in Northern Ireland, Margaret Thatcher, and Diana, Princess of Wales. It was simply inconceivable that she was dead. Whilst I have never been a Diana worshipper – and found some of the hysteria that followed pretty excruciating – the sudden tragedy of seeing a global icon being taken away in her prime, leaving two gorgeous boys motherless, was truly shocking.

So the atmosphere was a little strange at church. I think it was an open day of some sort, because I remember there being tea and cakes, but of course everyone was ruminating over what had befallen the Royal Family.

All Saints was a good 'starter' C of E for the uninitiated, as I was at that time. (Ed had been confirmed as an Anglican as a student, so was a little more au fait with the liturgy and traditions of the Church of England.) It was fairly informal with a small congregation, boasting a traditional morning service with communion, a family-based service with Sunday School, and a chilled evening service with acoustic worship and more challenging discussion. We initially frequented the evening service, until children dictated otherwise. In those glorious, lazy years BC (before children), we would spend all afternoon in bed, cuddling and listening to football on the radio. We would then dash across to church, hair still wet from the shower. No wonder we got so many knowing looks from the rest of the congregation!

It was at the 7 o'clock service that I was given the opportunity to teach the word for the first time, in 1998. This went so well, I was later asked to preach at the larger family service on a Sunday morning. This began a fourteen-year period in which, between kids, I preached and led services in the Church of England, initially at All Saints, then later at St Bartholomew's, where we moved to in 2002. All Saints enabled me to learn and perfect my technique, gradually developing a preaching style that mixed a hard-hitting Gospel message with my dry sense of humour.

It was while we were going to All Saints that I fell pregnant with our first child, Carter (the name runs in Ed's family). I can't say Carter was planned; it was more the result of a Christmas Eve cuddle without precautions! It must happen a lot, because the maternity ward was heaving at the end of September 1999 when Carter was born. I found the whole hospital experience terrifying; not so much the labour, which was long and painful but aided by an epidural when Carter started getting distressed. It was more the way you are left alone and to your own devices with an event that is entirely alien to you. And to add to that, your husband is sent away. Having Carter at 3 am meant that by the time I had been stitched up and sent up to the ward (200+ stitches on account of an awkward ventouse delivery) it was about 5 am. The cleaners came in about an hour later and then breakfast was served. Carter just screamed solidly the whole three or four days I was in hospital. He wouldn't feed properly and therefore wouldn't pee, which is the sign that the kidneys are functioning and allows mother and baby to return home.

Despite this fractious start to life, Carter grew into a good-looking child, with an impossibly cheeky smile, piercing blue eyes and a shock of white blonde hair. Two and a half years later, our daughter Kristen was born, another blonde-haired, blue-eyed model Aryan child. She would have been born on my birthday, as I was only in early labour on the actual day she was born. However, there was no way I was having a lifetime of joint birthday parties, so Ed and I took all the usual measures to precipitate labour. I drank pints of raspberry tea, we had a curry, had sex, but it was the high-speed drive along the country lanes near our house that finally did the trick! Four hours later, Kristen was born, another messy ventouse delivery with stitches, though not as hideous as first time round.

Officially Straight: The Housewife Years

She was a sleepy baby, or maybe, like us, she was simply exhausted by her big brother, who was turning into a real handful. We had to go to parenting classes to learn how to handle him, as we struggled to cope with his hyperactivity. Now we can see that he was just very clever, and it frustrated him no end being in a toddler's body. I remember visiting a friend with Carter whilst still pregnant with Kristen. The lady in question had a son as well, a few months older than Carter. After just ten minutes of observing Carter whirlwind around her front room, Justine remarked that it must be like having two children already!

Life trundled on in the manner familiar to all stay-at-home mums: attending mother and toddler groups that you *really* don't want to go to, but feel obliged to attend, in order to socialise your child and not become too isolated. The endless kids' birthday parties at the weekend were another feature, as well as all those interminable nativities, carnivals and pre-school events. By the time I had my third child, another son, in the late spring of 2005, I had really had enough of the mumsy stuff. Fortunately, David (DJ) was an easy baby, quite happy to tag along with his big brother and sister, so I didn't need to attend all the toddler groups with quite the same intensity. It was not cost-effective to go back to work, so I had to do the whole stay-at-home mum thing. I wrote fiction avidly to keep my brain active.

At that time, people were forever saying to me things like, 'don't they grow up fast' and 'enjoy it while you can, they aren't little for long!' While I am glad I did stay at home, because I was there for all the milestones, I cannot say that time flew by. It felt like for ever that I was bundling children into car seats, dealing with nappies and puddles, and coming up with cost-effective plans to keep the children occupied and happy.

One mumsy outing I won't forget, though, was a trip to Marks and Spencer in September 2001. A friend and I were just walking through the store, following an afternoon coffee with our two-year-olds, when we saw a huddle of people in the middle of the menswear department. We wondered what was going on and joined the throng.

As part of the Christmas display, the store had erected about nine television screens to form a giant screen on the wall. We were confronted with pictures of billowing smoke pouring out of the Twin Towers of the World Trade Center in New York. There was an air of hushed shock as we struggled to come to terms with what was going on in the news reel. People used to ask the question, where were you when you heard President Kennedy was assassinated or John Lennon had been shot? Now they ask, where were you when the Twin Towers came down? Well, I was in Marks and Spencer, Aniton Woods, on 9/11. Thirteen years later, I would visit Ground Zero in Lower Manhattan, staring down at the two giant squares in the ground where the towers had been, now converted into two memorial water features. They reduced everyone present there to silence, too.

My mother had reacted badly to the news that I was pregnant with DJ in 2004. While she could accept me having a second baby so that Carter would not be an only child, she really did not get why we would want a third. The fact that we already had 'one of each' (good job I didn't give birth to an intersex or trans child), made this decision seem even more foolish to her stress-averse ears. In fairness, she was not alone: a close friend had also advised me against having a third child, feeling it would be the straw that broke the camel's back. (I was not mentally strong at all at this point in my life.) In the end, I told her I wasn't going to apologise for falling in love with someone and wanting to have their babies, and that seemed to nip that particular issue in the bud. Relations gradually improved again.

In 2000, we had moved from the centre of Aniton

to Aniton Woods, a suburb seven or eight miles out of town. At first, we still commuted to All Saints, but it simply became too much of a drain on our energy and so we started trying out local churches. We adopted a 'three strikes and you're out' rule, trying a place three times and, if we still didn't like it, moving on. Having become rather Anglicanised by this point, I was used to a structured 15–20 minute sermon. So the local free church in Aniton Woods, with its patriarchal leadership team, shambolic sermons and interminable musical worship/ prayer ministry was ruled out. I swear that one week we went every single person on the stage was male, middle-aged and dressed in a burgundy shirt and chinos!

We finally ended up at a modern, evangelical Anglican church called St Bartholomew's. News of my gifting spread, and I was soon invited to speak at services – the evening service initially. I gathered a bit of a reputation for my sermons, so that more people than usual would come if they knew I was preaching. This did not go down that well with the vicar, himself a gifted preacher. However, I continued to flourish at St Bart's and started leading and preaching at the main Sunday service, as well as leading a midweek women's group. Occasionally I would get asked to speak at other churches and events, too, such as the Women's World Day of Prayer, a slightly old-fashioned global ecumenical event that upholds disadvantaged women in some of the poorest countries of the world.

In between the birth of Kristen and DJ, I got quite low in spirits again. I lost a lot of weight, which wasn't entirely unwelcome, but I look back at photos from that time, and wonder where my boobs went. Wherever they went, they've certainly come back now! The downturn in mood was a fairly nasty combination of my bisexual 'demons' and post-natal depression. It was exhausting looking after three young children with no family support. I would take them out, and just feel so sad inside when

I saw grandparents pushing buggies, or gamely tucking into soggy Big Macs with their grandkids.

Whilst my mum has always made the effort to visit and takes a genuine interest in the children, there was never any option of leaving the children with my parents for the weekend, let alone a week of the school holidays. I guess they just didn't feel equipped for the task, but it did result in the children spending much more time with their paternal grandmother when she was still alive than my parents. Despite being far older and considerably less mobile than my parents, we could always leave the kids with Granny S, and consequently they built a strong bond with her. In fairness to my dad, he doesn't keep in great health and travelling is a challenge for him. I guess it's not really their fault that I met a Londoner and chose to settle across the border, after all.

Ed has always been a brilliant, hands-on father, but he worked long hours and was shattered himself. We also had to deal with his mother's failing health and the realisation that we would need to move her from London, where she was not coping alone in a large four-bedroom house. Fortunately for me, I made some good friends in the locality, who did give me some of the support I needed. There were a couple of women from church who were fantastic at taking Carter or Kristen off my hands, so that I could get a bit of rest.

I also got very friendly with another mum who lived a few streets away. Serena became a very close friend and helped me no end. In the end I got a bit too emotionally dependent on her, to the extent that it felt like my world was caving in if she didn't reply to a text, or call me. Fortunately, we both realised what was going on before it was too late. The friendship was put on the back burner for a while as we both regrouped. Our children had grown apart as well, so it was difficult, but perhaps necessary, to give each other some space.

I nearly lost Serena a couple of years ago when she

suddenly contracted meningitis. But Ted, her husband, was an absolute hero, getting Serena to A&E in the nick of time. They pumped her full of antibiotics and she made a full recovery. It gave all of us a real fright and the sheer anguish I felt at the thought of losing her brought us close again, no explanations required.

Serena and I remain great friends. We both know we will always be in each other's lives and can totally rely on each other when the chips are down. Serena is one of those honest types whom you can utterly rely upon. I trust her implicitly and I know I will always love her deeply, no matter what life throws up. People like that, I have painfully realised as I traverse through life, are like gold-dust. As I always tell my kids, your friends are the people that actually help you and stick by you, not the people that are cool or popular or appear to say all the right things. All three of our children have solid friendships that have lasted for years, so I like to think I've brought some influence to bear on that.

The depression continued to rumble under the surface up to and including the birth of DJ in 2005. I alluded to the film *Four Weddings and a Funeral* earlier. We had experienced the wedding season, now it seemed to be time for less joyous events. For three Januaries in a row, someone in my friendship circle died. In 2002, we lost the worship leader at our last church, with whom Ed and I were very friendly, after he had a sudden heart attack. He was in his early fifties. We read the prayers at the large funeral that followed, me heavily pregnant with Kristen. In 2003, one of my closest friends from university, Marie, died of a brain tumour, aged just thirty-two. Then just one year later, Leona, a close friend from FOB who was also Carter's godmother, died from lung cancer – also in her early thirties – even though she'd never smoked a cigarette in her life. (Some years later, another close friend from my FOB cohort died of breast cancer at forty-one – incredible, really.)

I saw Leona in the hospice the afternoon she died; it was truly shocking to see this stunningly beautiful green-eyed brunette reduced to skin and bone, ravaged by that awful disease. It doesn't need to be the death of a family member to knock you for six. It's that confrontation with your own mortality that is often the painful part. And there was much looking death in the eye around that time.

It wasn't that I felt angry with God – I have never felt angry or resentful towards God, like many grieving people do – it was more that these untimely deaths caused me to re-evaluate my whole life. I began to feel that life was passing me by. It could have been me dead at thirty-two, having never achieved anything beyond what was biologically normal for women, and, perhaps more significantly, having never fulfilled the same-sex attracted side of my nature. These feelings sent me into a frenzy of conflicting emotions and I began to unravel. I found the children difficult to deal with and life just got too chaotic to handle. One particularly shambolic preaching performance in church saw me paid a concerned visit by the vicar. I was advised to take a step back from church stuff and to view my children as my mission over preaching the Gospel.

I now sense, with the benefit of hindsight, that it was not just one bad sermon that led to this advice. It was probably a combination of him being threatened by my popularity at church, and possibly some inkling that I was bisexual owing to a verbal indiscretion on my part somewhere along the line, as well as genuine concern for our welfare as a family.

In any case I took this advice, and became a 'backbencher' at church as I tried to establish some sense of order and routine at home. I continued to write to keep my brain active, self-publishing three throwaway novels between the years 2005 and 2009. I had some moderate success selling these locally, but it was never about fame or success. I just wanted to do something, anything, that represented some kind of legacy. The deaths of the two contemporaries of mine in particular had that effect on me.

I have always been prone to depression and mood swings – *mercurial* as more than one person has said about me. (I'll take mercurial over miserable any day.) In 2006, I realised that I was going rapidly downhill, so on the advice of friends, I finally bit the bullet and visited my GP. I had undergone a basic six-session counselling programme at the surgery a few years previously but not found it particularly helpful, so it was fair to say I was somewhat dubious about this course of action.

It's one of life's great misnomers, in my view, that it's always good to talk. What did Sven-Göran Eriksson once say to David Beckham? Words are like silver, but silence is golden ... I look back on the 'housewife years' and realise just how much time I spent dissecting (bi-secting?) my faith and sexuality to friends, clergy, counsellors, without it ultimately doing much good. More often than not, nobody had a clue how to help, and trained counsellors fell into that category as well. If they were Christian counsellors or pastoral support people, then they would trot out the standard line on adultery and the need to focus on my husband and kids, and just ignore the same-sex stuff *(Simples!)*. If they were non-Christian practitioners, then they didn't really get the faith side of things. I couldn't just come out the closet and express my bisexual feelings, like declaring a preference for vanilla ice cream. Not only was there a husband and children involved, but a whole church congregation! As for friends, some were very supportive, but more often than not I just alienated people. People had this picture of me as self-confident, witty and – by virtue of my marriage and three children – heterosexual and 'normal'. I think they somehow felt disappointed or cheated to know the real Jaime. I'm not sure whether it was my sexuality *per* se that was so off-putting, or my lack of discretion and my emotional incontinence in general at that time. Probably a combination of the three.

Looking back, there was, of course, absolutely no need to self-disclose or to be so indiscreet in general. I suppose it was currency for me. If I felt I wasn't getting enough attention or empathy from someone, I would play the bisexual card. I didn't really ever think about the effect this must have had on Ed – I was way too self-obsessed. To a certain extent, I have always resisted being normal. I always tell everyone who knows me, I can take most criticism but please don't call me boring or mumsy. To which the usual response is, don't worry, Jaime, you're neither!

I guess subconsciously I also hoped to garner support and love from people by 'coming out' to them, but it didn't usually turn out that way, and I would be left feeling foolish and vulnerable. I lacked self-esteem, I suppose, but that's what comes of not being allowed to be yourself, either growing up or in your replacement support networks, like the Church. There has never been a period in my life, up until very recently, where it has been all right to be *me*. It wasn't all right at home; it wasn't all right at church. It wasn't all right later on in LGBT gatherings – secular ones didn't appreciate my faith and Christian LGBT groups rarely cater for bisexual people who are married with children. Things are beginning to change for me now, but more about that later.

Basically, if you're not able to be yourself and make mistakes organically, at the age-appropriate time, you wind up making those errors later on in life. The problem with making mistakes as a fully fledged adult is that there's less understanding and forgiveness amongst your peers. Displaying a split personality and wayward emotions is acceptable in your teens and early twenties; less so in your thirties and early forties. People just think you're odd and avoid you.

The GP advised me to try medication this time, owing to the length of time I had been depressed, and I was prescribed fluoxetine (Prozac). After just a few weeks, it took effect and I began to feel better. The pressure of bringing up three children with little extended family support was in itself cause for low mood, let alone dealing with the confusing psychosexual situation I found myself in, as a married Christian bisexual.

Figures vary wildly online so I can't present you with any firm statistics, but it is generally thought that around one-third of Christian women in churches are currently taking, or have taken, antidepressant medication (typical SSRIs like Prozac, Zoloft or Paxil) at any one time. (Interestingly, the most elevated figures are among Mormon women in the State of Utah, where 70 per cent of residents are members of the Latter-Day Saints.) The pressure to pronounce that Christ is 'sovereign' and sufficient in our lives and to appear as strong, faithful Christian women means that all too many of us mask the real issues going on inside. As the psychologists tell us, we are only as sick as the secrets we keep. That's a hell of a lot of sick, anxious people in a place that purports to offer hope, joy and inner peace.

Ultimately, I did follow the 'Christian' course of action, and threw myself into my family and children, though with the secular assistance of antidepressant medication. To immerse myself in Ed and the kids has always been my default position when things get tough, and it generally works. Not because it's the right, Christian, *heterosexual* thing to do, but because Ed and the kids are the people who know me best, love me no matter what, and enable me to be me – which is healing in itself.

This will sound like a very strange statement, but the National Trust also helped save my sanity! For the uninitiated, the National Trust is a rather stuffy British organisation that protects listed buildings in the UK as well as forestland and coastline. You pay your rather hefty subscription fee, which gives you unlimited access to any NT properties in England, Wales and Northern Ireland,

and some in Scotland too, I believe. We spent many a Saturday at NT properties within ninety minutes' radius of our home, and whilst they might have complained at the time, the children are all very knowledgeable concerning social history and excel in the humanities at school.

The years where I wasn't so involved at church served as a hiatus for me and my mental health slowly recovered. I threw myself into family life and spent every weekend and every day of the school holidays driving the kids here, there and everywhere, to beaches, country parks, museums, farms ... you name it, we'd done it and bought the bendy pencil! I dread to think how much fuel I got through. It was not an environmentally friendly way to bring up kids – preserving our heritage whilst ruining the air quality – but it was good for my interior landscape.

I think, though, to a certain extent, we kind of overdid the whole day trip with picnic thing. It got to the point where my stomach would clench up if I went within sniffing distance of a Mint Club biscuit! We perhaps raised the kids' expectations by doing so much with them, to the point where they couldn't cope with just hanging out at home of a weekend. I also think that I didn't want to think about stuff too much, i.e. my sexuality. It was just easier to keep going with the kids until I ran out of energy and flopped into bed at night. That's not to say I didn't have 'dark nights of the soul' over my lack of female action, but I learnt to suppress these feelings through keeping busy with domestic stuff.

Sometimes Ed and I would watch a film with a gay theme, like *Brokeback Mountain*, and I would fall into a depressive mood. I tried during that time to avoid television programmes, books or films with homosexual content, as it would invariably send me into a pit of despair over the unexpressed side of myself, that side that longed to walk down the street hand in hand with a woman, or to snuggle up in front of the log fire with some older, wiser woman who would love me no matter what (cue soft-focus

Officially Straight: The Housewife Years

Hollywood imagery, with Cameron Diaz as me and Jodie Foster as my older woman … yeah right!).

Seriously, though, there were still evenings where I cried my eyes out into the pillow (once I was sure Ed was asleep), but I just swallowed it down in the morning, and, in the words of Winston Churchill, kept buggering on. KBO. (KBO was a popular maxim used by Winston Churchill to maintain morale during the war.) Churchill, I know, was also the owner of a large 'black dog' that refused ever to let him completely alone. So I was in good company.

Unsurprisingly, such self-imposed censorship affected my sense of identity, though admittedly, this is an experience common to most parents, not just LGBT ones. I remember one weekend in particular when a close mutual friend came to stay. She spent the entire weekend talking to Ed and shunning my company. I read too much into that and challenged her on it. She replied that she had no romantic feelings for Ed, it was just that she felt she didn't know me any more. She said that I had become the perfect housewife but was no longer the Jaime she knew and could relate to.

I think it's fair to say that I swapped one mask (church) for another (housewife). But that said, the 'decommissioned' years hold many precious memories, and I look back with great pride and nostalgia at all the places we went with the kids and the mutual bonds we forged as a family. Throughout this period, Ed was more than a rock – he was a whole mountain range. I got better largely through his unwavering love and support for me. Nobody knows me and understands me like Ed, and nobody has ever had the power to make me feel better in body and spirit than he has. He is so central to all that I am, that I've dedicated a chapter to our marriage later on.

5

The Broken Jug

I want to break with the constraints of chronology for now, to speak of an incident that was somehow prophetic in my life. I use that word 'prophetic' reluctantly, having seen it mightily abused and generally misused for wishful thinking during my charismatic church life. But prophetic it proved to be.

One morning circa 2005/2006, I had gone out for a coffee with my cultured friend, Janice. Like many women, I have friends for all occasions, a bit like handbags, really. At that time, Janice was my intellectual sparring partner, another friend Carolyn was my 'sex'[1] friend and Serena was my Claire Rayner! I had two of the kids with me, DJ in his buggy and Kristen on her reins (= *ersatz* straitjacket). Carter was at school by now. We went to a rather smart coffee house in Abbotts Green, a local market town popular with 'Ladies Who Lunch' and 'Christians who do Coffee'.

Prior to going for a drink, we mooched about the shops, spending some time in a charity shop that had a considerable collection of second-hand books. Janice probably had her nose in some obscure work of classical mythology, whilst I pounced upon a copy of the collective

---

[1] The friend you discuss naughty underwear and sexual issues with.

works of Heinrich von Kleist, a German dramatist I had studied at university. (That one sentence tells you precisely the calibre of charity shops in Abbotts Green. I swear I once saw diamonds on the dummy in the window display of the local Marie Curie!)

To return to Heinrich von Kleist – in my final year at SSU, I had starred in one of his plays, *Der Zerbrochene Krug* (*The Broken Jug*). This comedy focuses on a scandal in a local village. The broken jug in the play symbolises a loss of chastity or innocence, and the main characters are called Adam and Eve! Kleist's life was less comedic, ending in a shotgun suicide pact in 1811 with his terminally ill partner, Henriette Vogel, in what must be one of the earliest assisted suicides recorded.

The Kleist book was in great condition and so I purchased it out of sentimentality, as I had long since lost my dog-eared script for *The Broken Jug*. Janice and I then went to the café with the little ones. We found a table near a bay window. In the corner stood a large ornate jug, undoubtedly antique and about two and a half feet high. There were many nice artefacts in the café and I remember remarking to Janice that I would need to watch Kristen, as she was following in her hyperactive brother's footsteps, despite a sleepy start to life. I kept an eagle eye on her, but she seemed to be settled at the table, colouring and munching on a bag of crisps, while DJ sat strapped in his buggy. Janice and I were deep in conversation and I didn't notice Kristen get up. Suddenly we heard a loud crash as Kristen ran headlong into the jug!

It broke into shards. I'd like to say Kristen burst into tears, but I don't think she was that bothered, to tell you the truth. I'm ashamed to say I contemplated doing a runner, but Janice wouldn't let me, so I told the waitress what had happened, offering to pay for a replacement, as it was clearly beyond a dash of UHU. The waitress sniffily informed me that it wasn't replaceable and that she would have to speak to the proprietor. I left my phone number, but fortunately it was never followed up. I don't know what I thought I was going to pay for the damage with – magic coffee beans?

When I reflected on what had happened later, it occurred to me that it was beyond the realms of coincidence that my daughter breaks a jug just half an hour after purchasing a book containing the play with the same name. More ominously, however, what was I being told? Was this a warning that I was about to lose my 'chastity', or more worrying, that I would be brought before judge and jury like Eve and publicly shamed, as in the play?

This sense of foreboding was compounded by another weird thing that kept happening. As a sixteen-year-old, I had gone to see Bryan Adams at Birmingham NEC, supported by up-and-coming UK band T'Pau. At that point, T'Pau had just reached number one with their biggest hit, 'China in Your Hand', which would remain at the top for five weeks. T'Pau played a brilliant set and in some ways eclipsed Bryan Adams ... but not quite. ('Summer of '69' remains one of the best rock songs ever recorded, IMHO.)

I'm sure most of you will already be more than familiar with this 1980s classic, but if not, 'China in Your Hand' is a song about being careful what you wish for, because it might just come and bite you on the bum, big time. You might just push that little bit too far and find your world comes crashing down around you. I hadn't heard it in years, but suddenly everywhere I went this song seemed to be playing. I even stepped out the car one day to buy a parking ticket to hear it blaring from the radio of a car nearby. Coupled with the 'Wind' poem from all those years ago, I felt as if I was being warned about some danger that was heading my way. Whatever it was, it seemed to involve pain and brokenness.

6

A Licence to Preach

2009–2012

DJ started school in September 2009, initially for afternoons only, as he was a late 'spring chicken'. The writing thing hadn't quite taken off for me, as – typically for me – my books crossed too many boundaries, not fitting neatly into any genre in particular. One London publisher showed an interest but eventually turned my first novel down.

At any rate, it was my public speaking hat that was weighing most heavily on the hat stand. I was missing preaching, dare I say it, to an audience. I missed the intellectual stimulation of preparing a sermon and the adrenaline-filled buzz of delivering it and (egotistically) taking the plaudits afterwards. In my defence, the most exciting part of all was feeling that God had used me to demonstrate the love of Christ to others.

I was playing that 'Is it you, God?' game with myself, wondering if it was time to throw my hat back into the ring, or to remain in my comfort zone, pottering around at home where there was *always* enough to keep me occupied. The problem with the latter scenario was, I am a terrible housewife. I hate cleaning and dusting. Ironing is the devil's own concoction and as for sewing and mending ... I'd sooner stab myself with the embroidery scissors. I'm pretty good at what I call *Ready, Steady, Cook* style cuisine – making something cheap and delicious out of leftovers in the fridge – but the rest of the domestic goddess stuff is pure purgatory.

So finding something that got me out the house and stimulated my brain seemed the way forward. Weirdly enough, it was something a friend said in the viewing gallery at my children's swimming lessons that gave me the confirmation I was looking for. Roz was thinking of buying a horse for her children to ride, and, in typical madcap style – some would say downright irresponsible style – she had found a horse on eBay! I'm not sure if there's a special section of eBay like there is for cars – eNeigh? – but she had found a suitable horse.

The day before, Roz had driven to see Dobbin and its owners. When she saw the horse, it needed to be shod quite badly. As she explained to me, the horse had been left 'out to grass' in effect and had not walked on hard ground for some time. I don't know anything at all about horses – I can't stand that whole snobby Hannah Gymkhana scene – but I gather horses can be roadworthy as much as cars can be. And this old boy needed some new shoes before it could hit the road.

It hit me right between the eyes as Roz said this – I had been out to grass for too long. I needed to put my shoes back on and get back out there. If you don't operate from a faith perspective, you might query this rather whimsical mindset. But for those who do, you will know instantly what that feeling is like. You've been wrestling with something for weeks, maybe months, praying without any answers, then suddenly, *wham*, you have your answer, when you least expected it.

Later that week, I emailed Geraint Boyce, our curate at St Bart's, and asked if I could come and see him. The previous vicar had now left and we were in an interregnum as the diocese looked to appoint a new incumbent. This is often not done with any degree of urgency, as it saves the diocese money, the longer they drag their heels over an appointment. Of course, they will make the usual noises about spiritual discernment, but it sometimes has more to do with saving six months' salary and redecorating the vicarage than anything else.

I had always got on well with the curate, who grew up fairly close to my parents' home in South Wales. We had a shared heritage, even if I wasn't technically Welsh. He was also an amazingly inspiring service leader and preacher, full of original ideas and unorthodox methods. I met with him one Saturday morning at church. I told him I was feeling called back to church involvement, and what were his thoughts on this?

Geraint was blown away. It transpired that a few days before, he had met with his spiritual director to discuss the workload currently on his shoulders due to the interregnum. He had bemoaned the fact that he had to lead and preach at nearly every service, when there was a woman who was 'languishing' in the back row who was gifted at preaching (this person being me) and who delivered the most amazing prayers. It was remarkable that I had turned up that morning to tell him I wished to get involved again.

We then discussed potentially training for ministry, as the Diocese had cracked down on unlicensed lay preachers (hopefully not due to the dubious sermon I had preached a few years back!). Geraint had his misgivings about Reader training, which is less confusingly titled 'Licensed Lay Ministry' (LLM) in other dioceses. He was not the first clergy person to intimate to me that Reader training was not worth doing; that it was a way of getting free labour in the Church with no resulting kudos for the un-collared graduate of the scheme. Even the training was longer than it was for ordained ministry. (I also harboured a sneaking suspicion that it was a way of gainfully employing talented oddballs in the C of E, a theory borne out by some of the people I met from the various year groups at Reader training residentials!) Basically, as a Reader you can preach sermons, help serve at Communion but not preside. You can't take weddings, but you can take funerals. Perhaps I was one of those oddballs.

Geraint advocated going down the non-stipendiary route to ordination, like he had. I was unsure, but agreed to look into it further.

He asked if I had any issues with going for ordination. I took a deep breath and mentioned my sexuality. I had been at church there for some seven years, but it had never felt safe to talk about it – indeed, there had never been a forum for discussion of same-sex attraction full-stop. He asked some questions about whether Ed was aware and whether I was bisexually active. I said yes to the former, no to the latter, and he seemed satisfied. But he said to me very firmly, 'Do not, under any circumstance, mention it to anyone at Diocese.'

The upshot of this meeting was therefore this – I needed to consider either Reader training or ordination in order to be preaching at church again, and I was to keep well and truly schtum about my sexuality. Meanwhile, he would contact the Diocese and arrange for me to speak to a DDO, which stands for Diocesan Director of Ordinands – not Dungeons and Dragons Online. I think.

I spoke to the DDO, which was quite exciting if a little out of my comfort zone, though more on account of her poshness than her status. It was recommended that I embark upon a 'period of discernment' where I would meet with a vicar outside of my immediate local area to prayerfully work out my calling. It was also recommended I attend one of a number of information courses on discerning vocation. I got myself booked on a course run by CPAS (Church Pastoral Aid Society) at a venue not too far from home, which proved interesting if not conclusive. I had a one-to-one appointment with a spiritual advisor to chat over my sense of calling. Her advice in the end was that I would be selling myself short by training as a Reader, and that I was a clear candidate for ordination. This was an illuminating comment, as it showed in what esteem Reader training was held compared to ordained ministry. It was not the first time I had heard sentiments like this, despite the best attempts of the C of E to describe it as a distinct and separate ministry in its own right.

I then began meeting with a female vicar quite a way from my home. Over the course of a few months, I met with her at various locations to discuss my vocation. She felt, however, that I was a candidate for Reader training, not ordained ministry. I can't remember her logic, but I think she didn't sense a calling on my life and that I was probably too busy with the children to pursue the ordained path. So that was rather confusing, in the wake of the earlier comments from the woman at CPAS.

Another part of the discernment process involved taking a module of the actual Reader training course, to assess my academic aptitude. Clearly this was unlikely to be an issue, as I had a First-Class degree and a masters, as well as a Postgraduate Certificate in Education, but they had to follow protocol. So I did a term of Old Testament theology, at the end of which I had to write a 3,000-word essay. I chose to write about Isaiah and the Suffering Servant – and got top marks out of the whole group. The feedback was that it was the best essay the tutor had ever marked in the long time he had been training Readers, with 85 per cent being the highest mark he had ever given. I got several congratulatory emails from various bigwigs at Diocese, too. I think the subject matter helped.

When the process of discernment was over, I was invited back to speak to the DDO. It was their decision that, owing to my reluctance to leave the local area due to the kids' schooling, I was definitely not a candidate for stipendiary (salaried) ordained ministry. That left non-stipendiary ordained ministry or unlicensed lay ministry (Reader ministry). After a long chat, the DDO felt that it was better, given my hectic home life, to do Reader training, as I could always 'trade up' (my words but her inference) to ordained ministry at a later point. I obviously came across as disappointed, as she remarked on the fact, but I could see the logic in the argument and consented. Some people would undoubtedly argue that this decision was made on a sexist basis, but in fairness I did have a lot on my plate with the three children and I felt this recommendation was made on pragmatic grounds, rather than anything more sinister.

I was then invited to attend a Readership selection day. This involved speaking to various existing Readers then delivering a two-minute sermon. It became apparent during the round of discussions that these people had little concept of my life as a mother with three growing children. They seemed to be labouring under the illusion that you could tuck the kids up in bed at 7.30 pm and have the evening to yourself to devour the latest Tom Wright book and rustle up a sermon! None of these scenarios were in the least bit likely, I can tell you.

The two-minute talk went well, as I knew it would, because I'd already been preaching for over a decade, unlike most of the other candidates there. I had already perfected the art of delivering a sermon without appearing to look at my notes. So I was fairly sure I would be accepted, and in due course, I received a letter confirming this was the case. The Reader training course was taught through a local college, so it would start in the autumn at the beginning of their academic year.

One of the most interesting comments that emerged during that day was that I hadn't mentioned my husband in my spiritual journey timeline, an exercise we had to complete in advance and speak about to the interviewer. I don't think I mentioned the kids either. I suppose I saw it as a spiritual exercise, outlining my personal walk with God; I saw marriage and children as normal life events, rather than stages on a spiritual journey. Now that I have a far more embodied understanding of my faith, it goes without saying that Ed's input into my life is key and therefore of spiritual significance, as are the children. But I wonder if they read anything into that? I certainly made no mention whatsoever of my sexuality, and they didn't ask at all. It was assumed that since I was married with three children, I was heterosexual and therefore no threat to the C of E, with its ban on homosexual activity amongst licensed or unlicensed ministers.

My confirmation letter, interestingly, stated that there were clear signs that I was a candidate for ordination, but that Reader training was the most suitable path for now. Again, I got the impression that Reader ministry was viewed as inferior to ordained ministry or a stepping stone to greater things. This contrasted with the message we were given at the selection day, that Reader training was an important and distinct ministry of equal value.

My acceptance on the Reader training course was announced at church. I felt oddly underwhelmed and embarrassed as I was made to go down the front and receive a round of applause. It didn't ever feel really me – it wasn't so much the status thing, though I'd be lying if I said that didn't come into it – it was more that Reader felt such a nondescript term, and something for older folk. I remember that I had worn really mumsy clothes that morning as well – a long flared denim skirt and a green round-necked top that made my boobs look enormous. I hadn't been expecting to be called down to the front, or I would have worn something less 'earth mother'!

Later that year, I attended the licensing service for the new vicar at St Bart's. As the readers walked in after the clergy, in their blue tippets and white choir gowns, I remember thinking 'I'm so glad I'm not doing that'. Then I realised I was … it was rather telling. The one thing that immediately strikes you when you see a gathering of Readers (I'm not sure what the collective noun is – a subservience of?) is how much older they tend to be than your average clergy. It unfortunately gives the impression that Reader training is for retired people at a loose end. At thirty-nine that made me feel like a bit of a failure, to be entirely honest, however the Diocese tried to spin the value of this ministry.

I began my training in the 2010/11 academic year. This meant I could officially start preaching and leading services at church again, though in reality I already had my feet under the table on that score, since Geraint was fine with me being involved whilst I discerned my vocation. I also helped serve at communion, not something I have ever enjoyed doing, though I'm aware it's a privilege and responsibility. I soon became totally immersed in church life once more, and was very much seen as part of the church leadership. My academic training served me well; I continued to get high marks in all the modules, and my assessed sermon at church was very well received.

My cohort was very small that year, and seemed to keep shrinking until there were just seven of us. We all got on exceptionally well, though we were so, so different. I was by far the most 'street' of all the trainee Readers, though, and also the most ignorant of church tradition and liturgy. By and large, the tutors liked my outspoken comments and lack of reverence for church tradition; I think they found it a welcome change (ovine behaviour and sycophantism is rife in the Church). I was one walking 'fresh expression' of the Christian faith! I still, to this day, do not understand what Rogation Sunday is, and isn't Compline something you add to your coffee when you've run out of milk? And don't even get me started on church choirs or clergy in hooded albs (the diocesan branch of the Ku Klux Klan had frightened the living daylights out of me at one Reader training weekend!).

I did not talk about my sexuality, though I made it clear what side of the tracks I was on theo-politically. One of the other students had a daughter who had recently had a civil partnership service, obliging him to walk her down the 'aisle' of the Registry Office. He had mixed feelings about this; everyone's eyebrows were raised when I defended her quite vehemently.

I witnessed an incredible amount of ignorance concerning gay issues in the Church of England, let alone awareness of bi or trans issues. In one of my training modules held at a local Anglican church, one of the leaders of the host church interrupted our session to ask advice of another church member who happened to be on my course. The said woman was in a state of high flux, as two women (who were *clearly* lesbians) had turned up at the introductory Alpha supper being held in the next room! What should she do? 'Welcome them as you would everyone else', came the dry response from her more enlightened church colleague. I think the woman in question was all but ready to don an Ebola-style contamination suit.

That's what total immersion in church life does for you. It's a pseudo existence that shields you from the realities of life and creates homogeneity in social circles. This blatant display of homophobia happened as recently as 2010. But the realities of life were about to hit me, with a vengeance.

7

Hole in the Sidewalk

2011–2013

In 2011, I began to fall into that trap that ensnares many a church leader – I started believing in my own importance (or 'ministry' as the Church likes to call it). I was heavily involved in leading services and preaching and had been entrusted with the planning and delivery of several prestigious services, such as Good Friday and the Nativity service. All these services had gone well, with my 'under the skin' sermons gaining me plaudits from the congregation and ordained clergy alike. I was a good all-rounder, as I could engage with adults at a deeper level, yet I was also at ease with children thanks to my experiences as a mother and parent helper at school.

I was also delivering the talk at several Alpha evenings. As we enjoyed relative freedom at St Bart's, the Alpha speakers were not required to use the official Alpha script contained in the leader's pack, so long as the main ideas were covered. I have to say, I have never liked Alpha. It smacks of the fundamentalist need for closure, for binary structures and consumerist packaging. We've got Jesus' death sorted; now let's move on to the Holy Spirit.

Alpha invites people to come along and ask the questions about Christianity they really want answers to, yet the subjects covered – whilst (arguably) central to the

Christian faith and church culture – are not central to the average person's life. I don't think I once wondered how and why I should pray as a non-believer, but I did want to know why God created wasps, menstruation, tonsils, homosexuality and Port Talbot.

In addition, the Church is generally so paranoid about either awkward questions or awkward silences, that they invite half the church along to bolster numbers. The net result of this is that 'newbies' are often drowned out by church members spouting the official party line, or feel too intimidated to ask what they want to know, for fear of looking stupid in front of all these apparently very knowledgeable believers.

For all my cynicism, Alpha did offer me another opportunity to do what I liked doing best – dressing up in a (short) black skirt and jacket and strutting around with a headset on, preaching the Word, making people think and making people laugh. As the last vicar had put it, 'You're good with words, and you know it!'

Looking back, I *was* pretty vain. Okay, very vain. I would spend ages getting ready for church whenever I was involved in services, making sure I looked slimmer, younger and sexier than any of the other women in the worship team. My perfectionist streak was never more pronounced than when I was planning a sermon. I had to be cleverer and funnier and more original than everyone else. Not for me a run-of-the-mill yawnsville talk on the 'Armour of Faith' or 'The Lost Sheep'. My natural showmanship and ability to project my voice enabled me to perform with confidence and carry it off with aplomb. It also meant I got a certain degree of adulation from impressionable people.

Like Penny. She had arrived at our church a year or two before with some fanfare, coming to faith via the Alpha course run at St Bart's. In fairness to Penny, the church makes such an almighty fuss whenever *anybody* comes to faith through Alpha that it is pretty much impossible *not* to be passed around church like a trophy within a nanosecond of praying the Prayer of Commitment.[1] To be honest, I had avoided her thus far; I was a little wary of her for a variety of reasons, not least on account of her vivacity.

Once I started leading services and preaching again on a regular basis, it became impossible for me to evade Penny. She would approach me after every service I was involved in and eulogise over my talks. To a certain degree, I was aware that she just wanted to be seen with me. I was central to pretty much all that was going on, and popular with most of the congregation. But it became apparent to me that she, at best, sought approval from me, at worst, had a bit of a thing for me. She was married with a child, but my gaydar/bi-dar was going off big time.

I received cards and emails which could have been interpreted as deep admiration, but I could recognise purple prose when I read it – probably because I was guilty of it myself at times. I ignored it as first; I found it a little over the top and she was an unknown quantity after all. But there was something about her, and it was flattering, and so I convinced myself there was no harm in extending the hand of friendship to this insecure woman, just a few years younger than myself. She made me laugh, and this has always served as a magnet for me. I had no intentions of offering anything other than a hand at this point, though I was aware that I found her attractive. So, against my better judgement, both as a married woman and someone in a leadership position in church, I encouraged her attention and engaged her in conversation.

Penny and I just clicked. We could talk for hours; she was smart and witty and we were of a similar age, so had cultural reference points in common. There was also, clearly, more than a degree of attraction between us. A flirtatious relationship soon developed between us and I suggested that we went out for a drink in the New Year, to get to know each other better as it was always hard to talk

---

[1] Typically after Talk 3 of the official Alpha course.

with kids around us. Looking back on it, it was really quite scandalous that we flirted so openly with one another in a church setting, and perhaps even more scandalous that I genuinely thought I could play with fire and not get burned – and that I did so with so little consideration for either of our husbands. But probably most scandalous of all was that I was in a position of leadership and should not, under any circumstances, have been fraternising to this degree with a congregant. Yes, I was stressed and bogged down with cares and worries at home and struggling with another onset of depression, but at the age of forty, I should have known better. Whilst I don't think any of the congregation at St Bart's would have recognised a Sapphic seductress if they'd run across the altar in a strap-on, brandishing the latest Sandi Toksvig book, I had no such excuse. I may have kidded myself that I could just be friends with this woman two years my junior, but I was fully aware from day one that there was an attraction between us.

This marked the start of what was to become the most traumatic event of my life, an event so painful that it's only now, three and a half years on, that I feel sufficiently healed to recount the story again. That said, I totally underestimated the deep pain and shame I still carry inside, which has risen like some kind of monster from the deep as I edit these chapters. It has been an immensely difficult process revisiting the events of spring 2012. I remain deeply ashamed of my behaviour, both as a wife and mother, but particularly in my capacity as a respected member of the church leadership team at that time. If you're not into church disciplinary process, then by all means skim past this. If you *are* intrigued by how the Church of England deals/can't deal with issues surrounding sexuality, then read on.

Lest you be in any doubt, *I wholly acknowledge and accept the impropriety of my behaviour*, and I remain scarred by the shame to this day. Nevertheless, of particular note, from both my perspective and those watching on at the time, was how overblown and draconian the reaction of the Diocese was to ten minutes of mutual stupidity by two consenting adults. Names and places have been changed to protect the identity of all those involved and, writing as a wife and mother, I would like to think readers would respect the rationale behind this.

As I stated in the introduction to this biography, I have no axe to grind with specific people or organisations. To remain in bondage to anger is no life at all, and I am far from blameless in the whole episode, in any case. I am not a person who bears grudges and neither do I harbour unforgiveness towards any one individual. I may never wish to clap eyes on certain people again for my own equilibrium – and I am sure the feeling is mutual – but there is no animosity on my part towards the people in question. Whilst I generally reject that disembodied notion of 'loving the sinner, hating the sin', in this case it holds a degree of truth. Though I cannot say, hand on heart, that I love the Christians involved, I certainly don't hate them. What I do find very difficult to countenance, however, is their attitude towards me and my LGBT brothers and sisters. I have angsted long and hard over these chapters, deciding what to include, what not to include. At the end of the day, there is no way of telling my story without reference to true events. It is my hope and my prayer that my honest intentions are apparent and no hurt is caused. I have done everything I possibly can to preserve the anonymity of people and places, and in so doing I hope it is abundantly clear that revenge or retribution do not feature on my radar, but rather a heartfelt desire to share my experiences as a bisexual Christian, because there's nothing else out there for bi people like us as I write.

This is no form of revenge, neither is it a confession. I've all but confessed myself out of existence in any case; I think I still bear the chafe marks from the sackcloth. Rather, this account is about demonstrating what a corner the Church has backed itself into over human sexuality and what damage is done to individuals, at a truly visceral level – whatever their status – through its passive-aggressive, ill-informed approach. But over and above that, it's about raising awareness of bisexuality and of the immense damage done to bisexual people (and sometimes *by* bisexual people) because of widespread ignorance of the orientation.

I wish to point out that this account is told entirely from my personal perspective and experience. Inevitably others will have a different take on events and there is undoubtedly a degree of myopia on my part regarding my own culpability. However, I believe myself to be an essentially honest and gracious person and I hope this is reflected in the narrative that follows.

So to return to January 2012 … I arranged to go out for a drink with Penny and we proceeded to enjoy a lovely evening, just two friends getting to know each other, discussing children and families. I have elected to remove much of the mutually embarrassing detail I originally included in this section, but suffice to say, Penny made it abundantly clear that she had feelings for me through verbal and physical gestures, and I likewise.

We carried on as friends for a while. There was always a borderline romantic element to our meetings, but we continued to pray and have fun together and it remained platonic. However, when we met to chat and pray towards the end of February, Penny was in tears, and said she had to be really careful because she had very deep feelings for me, and loving me perfectly would be a challenge (we were reading 1 John 4 about perfect love, which seems deeply ironic now). She never actually said she was in love with me or that she was bisexual so I didn't feel I could ask her outright, but it was implied and she inferred that she had had some form of relationship with women in the past. I should have seen warning signs here, but it was just so great to have a funny, clever friend my age to pray with and socialise with. I suppose I turned a blind eye to the mutually strong feelings we obviously had for each other. Life was full of stresses and cares at that time; Penny provided some welcome warmth and colour to my rather grey existence at that point in time.

On another occasion, Penny told me that she had always needed to be intimate with women, but that it wasn't sexual. I agreed that I was also tactile with women sometimes, but that this was not sexual, and agreed with her that this was difficult to explain to people. I guess we were both somewhat in denial, because even though no sexual activity took place, there was definitely a frisson between us. I craved spending time alone with her, though I honestly had no intention of sleeping with her in the full sense of the word. I wanted kisses, cuddles, hearts and flowers – in short, some fun and some TLC from another woman, rightly or wrongly. I wanted to take her to beautiful places, spend the weekend together without those pesky kids, drink the bar dry, laugh ourselves hoarse … in short, more than a friendship, but less than an affair.

I was indiscreet, I was naïve and – as it panned out – entirely deluded, but I had no overt sexual designs on her and, to be perfectly blunt, I don't 'do' downstairs with women, a point I was subsequently to make to the diocesan investigation team. (They weren't too enamoured with my open acknowledgement of this; indeed, they struggled with my openness throughout.) The underlying issue, looking back on the events of that time, was my poor mental health and lack of boundaries, which is not to excuse my behaviour but simply to put it in context. But it is very hard to draw boundaries around an identity and human reality that is never acknowledged, let alone psychologised, evaluated, documented or discussed by the ruling body – in this case, the Church. There is no ethic on how to exist as a bisexual Christian, no Grove booklet on the subject, and therefore no informed support. All I knew was that pretending to be straight and repressing the same-sex attractions raging inside of me

Hole in the Sidewalk

(as recommended by the Church of England's own treaty, *Issues in Human Sexuality*[2]) was making me ill, very ill. It was affecting my marriage, my mental health, my energy levels and, most importantly, my ability to parent my three precious children. It was blatantly obvious to me that Penny was suffering from the same malady as a wife and mother. In that sense, I would argue we were both victims of ignorance and apathy on the wider Church's part, though I chose to challenge it, whereas she colluded with the system.

We continued to see each other and pray together. We had a particularly lovely day when I took Penny and her daughter to a local history museum. I remember her telling me that day that she loved me deeply and never wanted to do anything to hurt me or stress me out, which of course seems deeply ironic now. There were many mutual declarations of love, which now seem absurdly hollow. We were like immature teenagers, rather than mature wives and mothers.

The kiss that changed things happened on 12 March. It happened during a powerful prayer session at her house. As we – ironically – gave thanks to God for our friendship, it became quite emotional. We clutched onto each other. Then out of nowhere, we kissed on the lips (but not inside the mouth). It was not instigated by either one of us and I certainly didn't plan it; it happened spontaneously. At no point did we go 'inside clothes' or touch each other beyond the kisses and hugs. By this time, it was nearly school run time and I had to go. Again, it does not feel appropriate to go into details, but Penny made it very clear that what had just happened between us had been amazing, a clear answer to the issue that had tortured her all of her life. She now knew for sure that she liked women, using the word 'delicious' to describe me.

[2] See p.42 for the 119 words used to summarise bisexuality in *Issues in Human Sexuality* (Church House Publishing, 1991).

As I drove home, I realised that while this may have felt wonderful, it was entirely inappropriate. I started to panic. I texted Penny a few times but she didn't reply. Later that evening, she called. She said the kiss and cuddle shouldn't have happened and that she was in a really bad place. She added that what happened had not come from her brain, but from somewhere else. I apologised for my part in it, she apologised for hers. She told me she couldn't ever go there again, that it was 'the road to hell'. This expression caused me a great deal of distress; I knew I had behaved badly for a whole host of reasons, but nevertheless I found this comment deeply offensive and homophobic. It cut me to the core.

That evening I told Ed what had happened. He forgave me immediately. I cried and cried and he stayed up all night talking things through with me. As ever, he was amazing, able to rise above his own hurt and give me the comfort and support I so needed. I knew then, as I know now, that I am not worthy of his unswerving love and devotion. The next morning, I sent an email of apology to Penny. I felt responsible for what happened, not because it was in any way one-sided, but because in my leadership role (let alone as a wife and mother), I should have known better than to have got myself in to such a situation.

A few days later Penny and I chatted it through after the Lent course at church, which I had been facilitating as part of the church leadership team. We both agreed to overlook it and resolved to do better. A week or so later, I got a text from Penny, saying that she didn't want any contact with me for a few weeks. I think she had visited some kind of spiritual healing ministry in the north of the county that morning. I got the impression, though she didn't tell me explicitly, that it was some sort of gay reparative therapy organisation.

This saddened me, as I have long since come to the conclusion that such outfits are inherently damaging to already vulnerable individuals struggling with largely immutable sexual identities. However, it was perhaps indicative of the internal turmoil Penny must have been experiencing concerning both her own sexuality and what had transpired between us. I sincerely regret the pain I must have caused her through my own lack of self-control and irresponsible behaviour. I was in a position of trust and leadership and should have had the strength to rebuff her overtures, whether consciously or unconsciously intended. Not only did my actions impact on her marriage and family life, but she would later be ostracised in church circles by those close to me, as details of our indiscretion and her response to this became known. I was so consumed by my own pain that I had little appreciation at the time of the agony she must have been going through herself.

However, while I could accept that we needed to give each other space, I felt it was out of hand when she blanked me at church the next Sunday. So I went downstairs during the Peace and said 'Peace be with you, Sister'. She had a hard, angry look in her eyes, and it was at that point that I realised she was not the person I had made her out to be – there was something inherently malevolent about the look she gave me. It was one of those expressions that almost sends you reeling backwards from the force of it. Perhaps I deserved it; it's hard to judge your own culpability in messy matters of the heart. I just remember that I felt frightened; I can recall that quite clearly. That look sent chills up my spine, not just because it was frightening in itself, but because I knew I was in trouble, owing to my leadership role in the church. Deep trouble. Some would undoubtedly argue that I deserved all that came to me, including her anger and rebuff. But that incident still shocked me.

During this very painful time for me, I confessed what had happened to three senior people at church whom I trusted implicitly: Lynda Hope, the female church warden; my home group co-leader, Nadine Scott; and Hillary

Norris, who was exploring ministry at that point and had become a good friend. I also made an appointment with a spiritual director outside of the Diocese, as I could see clear confidentiality issues in chatting to Ann McVeigh, my spiritual director at that time, who also went to St Bart's. Our vicar, Roy Littlecombe, was taking some time out, so I couldn't talk to him. Geraint was consequently hectically busy and I didn't want to bother him, though, if I'm honest, I probably used this as an excuse not to confide in him. Sexuality issues were totally taboo at St Bart's, as they are within most Anglican churches, and I just felt plain awkward at the thought of talking to either Roy or Geraint about what had happened.

If you're an outsider to mainstream church culture in the UK, you might find this utterly unbelievable, but I cannot over emphasise just how taboo *any* discussion of human sexuality was, and still is, in large numbers of our churches. Nobody *ever* talked about homosexuality, let alone bisexuality, at church while I was there. It was even avoided during Alpha, which purports to be a forum for people exploring the faith to ask questions about life. Clergy are not adequately equipped or grounded in concepts relating to human sexuality, as a passing glance at *Issues in Human Sexuality* will tell you. That this thin and now quite elderly glorified pamphlet represents the sole mandatory literature ordinands are required to read on the complex and ever-evolving subject of sexuality tells you much about the priority church hierarchies give those who do not fit into the heterosexual gender schemata. I did not feel able to speak to any of my clergy colleagues in the leadership team about what had happened. This was not only due to the cringe factor, but also because, frankly, I did not feel that a single one of them, male or female, would have possessed the knowledge and insight to support me and offer me (informed) wise counsel.

With hindsight, not telling a member of the clergy about what had happened between Penny and me was extremely foolish. But you have to understand that there was no space or opportunity *whatsoever* for discussing LGBT issues at St Bart's or indeed within my Reader training sessions. There was an altar cloth of silence over the whole subject of same-sex attraction – probably a purple cloth at that. It was the ecclesiastical equivalent of discussing porn with your great aunt.

I finally had a civilised conversation with Penny on Good Friday. I was leading and preaching at the Good Friday service. After the service, she fell in step beside me as we took part in the Walk of the Cross to the local shops, where we would meet with other Christians from the surrounding area for a short open-air act of worship. We apologised to one another for losing the plot and mutually acknowledged that we had lost sight of God for a while. She told me that she had taken my advice and had told her husband about her sexuality and that he had been all right about it. Penny then stated that she felt her attraction to women was a genetic flaw, a weakness, an addiction akin to alcoholism. I replied that I didn't feel like that; it was part of me and something I had to acknowledge and adapt to, though there were obviously right ways and wrong ways of going about it – my way of acknowledging that I had made errors and wanted to move on. I warned her against making herself ill by either bottling up her sexuality or by throwing herself into a frenzy of church activity to avoid thinking about it – both mistakes I'd made in the past. She wanted to talk further, but we were both away for the next two weeks, so there would be no opportunity.

It ended amicably, with Penny chatting and laughing with me, my husband and mutual friends. It felt as if we'd tied up loose ends and obtained a large degree of closure. A few weeks later, I discussed with my friend Hillary the need to confess what had happened to either Geraint or the Bishop, in the vicar's absence. But I had left it too late.

8

A Living Nightmare
2012–2013

Thursday 26 April 2012 was the worst day of my life. It started with a phone call from Geraint Boyce. Geraint never made phone calls unless it was serious. He liked to e-pastor, due to significant work and family commitments. I think deep down I knew what was coming. It didn't stop me losing control instantly when he stated that he had received an email from Penny. He didn't state exactly what it said but that she had made an allegation of sexual advances against me. I can't remember his exact words because it was all a teary heart-stopping blur at the time. But he was dismayed when I confirmed that there had been a kiss, albeit only one kiss. I think he wanted to hear that she had made it all up. His voice was cracking and he told me that this was awful for him, too. Geraint indicated that he had also had a phone call about this from Dorothy Flint, a licensed Reader at our church, the night before.

He informed me that he would need to come round either that evening or Friday evening. Ed was away on business in Gloucester, but nevertheless I said it would have to be tonight, because there was no way that I could sleep or function anyway. He asked if he could bring Dorothy Flint. I said absolutely not, because of her known right-wing conservative views. I got on well with Dorothy, but I knew we didn't see eye to eye on sexuality and couldn't see how she would be a comforting presence. So I asked instead for my friends from church – Nadine Scott or Hillary Norris – to accompany him, as they already knew what had happened between Penny and myself, as did Ed.

The rest of the day was one big painful blur as I was alone while the children were at school. In the evening the children were shipped off to my mother-in-law's under the pretext of an important church meeting. Hillary and Nadine arrived just after Geraint and we all sat in the living room. Geraint looked terrible. He began proceedings by stating that I was loved and valued by all at St Bart's and that that would never change. He explained that he had been obliged to phone Bishop Andrew for advice in the absence of Roy Littlecombe as priest-in-charge. The Bishop had informed him that the matter should be escalated up to him, and that Geraint was not to be involved in any capacity other than reading out a statement. At that point I knew it was going to be bad. Nadine held my hand, Ed sat on the floor opposite looking furious. Geraint pulled out his Blackberry and proceeded to read out a statement from Bishop Andrew stating that due to allegations of 'unwanted sexual advances' made by Penny against me, I was to be removed from LLM ministry (Reader training) with immediate effect. I was not to be involved in preaching or leading services or to attend that Saturday's Reader training day. Sunday's service, which I was due to lead, would be assigned to someone else. Both Penny and I would be interviewed separately by senior clergy from the Diocese and I should expect a phone call in the next day or so.

We all let out a stunned gasp, I shrieked and from that point on cried uncontrollably. Hillary immediately moved to my sofa and held my other hand. Both Hillary and Nadine expressed astonishment and abject horror at the allegations. They trusted me and believed my version of events, which I had already shared with them weeks ago. Whilst I am a naïve idiot who wears her heart on her sleeve at times, I am not prone to deceit and dishonesty, and they knew that. Ed was livid; I was hysterical. I can't remember much else about the evening, except that Geraint had to sit there in silence, as instructed. He said he had been told by the Bishop to leave immediately, but that from a humane and pastoral perspective he couldn't bring himself to do that. They all left together about an hour or so later. On leaving, Geraint loosened his dog collar and gave me a hug. I appreciated the gesture immensely.

The allegations were *not* representative of the mutual experience Penny and I had shared and I wondered what on earth had happened in the interim period for her to choose to make allegations that she must have known would devastate me and my family. I had flirted with her; I had made foolish declarations of affection; I had made hearts and flowers gestures; I had behaved entirely inappropriately as a wife, mother and church leader, but one-sided sexual advances? I was astounded that someone who had claimed to love me so deeply, who had kissed me and called me 'delicious', could have done such a thing to me, with no warning, and – to add insult to injury – by the cowardly method of email. My health began to deteriorate in the days and weeks following the allegations; I couldn't sleep and lost several kilos in weight.

The next few days following the meeting with Geraint were unspeakably awful. There was no phone call on Friday from anyone at Diocesan House and so I had to stew all weekend. I didn't sleep. Because of the three children, we had to go through the motions of being all right. Ed told them I was under the weather to explain why I kept hiding under the duvet or fainting from lack of food and sleep. I couldn't eat, despite Ed's best attempts to buy me my favourite treats. I remember him trying to force-feed me cheese scones, but I just couldn't keep any food down.

The Sunday morning was particularly hard, knowing Geraint was leading the service for which I was on rota. I had spent all the week before preparing a humorous PowerPoint show and I just kept thinking *what a waste*. Ironically, Ed spent the morning fixing the marital bed which had started sagging in the middle as the slats weren't screwed in tightly enough. That seems particularly poignant now. I spent the rest of the weekend putting together a statement of what I believed had happened between Penny and myself because I knew I might well be too upset and incoherent when they interviewed me.

On Monday I couldn't be left alone on mental health grounds, so I went to Nadine's house in Crofton Abbott. (Nothing I write here can possibly express just how amazing Nadine Scott was, and is. I love that woman so deeply, but it's just too painful to meet up with friends from that time.) During the morning, I finally received a phone call on my mobile from the Revd Susannah Fulwell from the Diocese. I was shaking all over as I took the call. She was very kindly in manner and said I would need to come to Diocesan House for 'a chat' with her and the Revd Canon Martin Langley about what had happened. Martin Langley was in charge of Reader training for the Diocese while Susannah was the Diocesan Director of Ordinands who had overseen my ministry discernment process. She was very reassuring and said it was nothing to worry about and that no one was judging me, or words to that effect. She said she was holding me in her prayers and we proceeded to arrange a meeting for the next day that fitted around school hours. I told her there was no way I was coming without my husband. She sounded slightly taken aback at this but consented.

Ed managed to work from home the next day, so that we could go to Diocesan House that afternoon (1 May).

I couldn't have driven there alone, as I was physically and mentally shot. When we got there, we were shown upstairs to the boardroom by Susannah's secretary. It didn't feel like the setting for a friendly chat – it was the same room I had sat in for assessed biblical exegesis several times at Reader training residential weekends.

Susannah came in first. She was friendly towards us. Canon Martin Langley came in a few minutes later. He looked grim and took a seat opposite me. Ed had strategically sat at a right-angle to me so that he could catch my eye and take over from me, should I be too upset to read my account. Susannah took a seat at the far end of the table and it was clear her role was to make notes and play second fiddle. It felt very cold, very formal and nothing like a friendly chat about what had happened. Martin then began by saying that this was difficult for all of us, and by the nature of what was alleged, difficult questions would need to be asked. Susannah opened in prayer. I was shaking all over and started to cry. For the rest of the interview I was in tears, or on the brink.

I can't remember the exact order of what happened next, but I was allowed to read out my statement. Martin let me read this uninterrupted, though it took me ages as I had to keep stopping to blow my nose and regain composure. I was at least grateful that he allowed me this opportunity. He did stare at me unflinchingly the whole time I was reading. I found this unnerving and terrifying. I felt as if he was trying to assess whether I was telling the truth or not, as well as listening intently. I suspected he didn't believe me. Though he was courteous and professional, he did nothing to put me at ease.

As the questioning began, I started to feel deeply uncomfortable at both the direction the questions were taking and that it was Martin asking them, since he was one of my course tutors as well. I wondered how on earth I was going to sit in a lecture or across the dinner table from him at residential weekends again, once the questions became sexual in nature. Naïvely, I still thought I would return to my Reader training at some point.

I tried to explain what I understood by sexual versus romantic versus platonic, but he didn't appear to be sympathetic to the diverse degrees of friendship between women. (I now regret the way I handled this whole discussion, because I don't think I did my cause any favours, but I was unwell and not wildly articulate that day.) Susannah appeared more understanding on this issue and, at that point, I wished she had been conducting the main interview instead of Martin. I tried to explain that the relationship with Penny was romantic rather than sexual but Martin was not interested in shades of meaning. Looking back, I think flirtatious was probably the right word, but like I said, emotional intelligence was not my strong suit at that point in time. It was sexy without being sexual, if that makes sense? However, whether it was romantic, flirtatious, sexy or sexual, it was certainly ill-advised and stupid, and I acknowledged as much.

At this juncture Martin asked permission to ask more intrusive questions. We agreed, because I didn't really feel I had an option and because I like to be honest and transparent. (I am now learning that discretion can be a greater and wiser virtue.) I don't remember exactly what he asked, but I know it related to our married sex life. Ed confirmed that there were no worries on that score, that we had an active and fulfilling sex life. It is all a bit of a humiliating blur, but I know it must have got quite intimate because I remember denying that I had genital sexual intentions towards Penny because I don't do oral sex with anyone, male or female, and that I wasn't into naked bodies. I know I told them I was a 'top half only' bisexual – as if such an admission would have helped my cause. It didn't appear to make a blind bit of difference that I had never taken my clothes off and spent the night with anyone other than my husband, that I was a virgin when I married (aged twenty-five) and had not slept with anyone else in fifteen years of marriage. The fact that I was more chaste than nearly everyone I knew, single or married, counted for nothing; I had kissed and flirted with someone of the same sex and that was enough to hang me. I know of straight married ordained clergy who have gone significantly further and held onto their jobs, so the argument that it was my marital or leadership status that was the issue, and not my sexuality, does not entirely wash with me.

I was asked if 'this sort of thing' had happened before. I confirmed that I had been emotionally close and cuddly to women before but not kissed or slept with them, which Ed confirmed. Martin asked if this was likely to happen again. Ed interjected at that point and said no more likely than he would get too close to someone either. I deeply appreciated the point he made. He was immensely loyal throughout. It was very clear to me that they had absolutely *no* idea what to do with me. I wasn't gay, but I wasn't wholly straight. My marriage was not in trouble and my husband was supportive of my sexuality. I did not fit a single box they sought to put me in. In short, I was an inconvenience – and a major one at that.

We then talked about my future. I stated that I loved my Reader training and that I didn't want to have to give it up. Martin said he couldn't make any promises which way the Bishop would go but that the interests of St Bart's would need to come first. We were told the Bishop should make a decision within a week to ten days, once he had received both interview transcripts. If Bishop Andrew couldn't come to a decision, it might be escalated up to the diocesan bishop, Robert. This felt very serious and terrifying. I could not believe that what had actually happened between Penny and me was so shocking and so complicated to sort out.

(I should add that, at no point prior to this meeting, or following it, did I have sight of Penny's allegations against me, beyond the banner headline. Had this been a court of law, I would have been allowed to defend myself adequately. But later on, when I heard some of the extreme comments she had made about me to Geraint Boyce, I was glad that I hadn't seen a transcript of any description. I think it would have tipped me over the edge. Perhaps I should give the Diocese the benefit of the doubt; maybe they were protecting me. On the other hand, it added to the whole sensation that I was 'guilty till proven innocent'.)

Susannah did enquire after my health and I told them that I was taking antidepressants and sleeping pills and was under the care of my GP. (Given this knowledge, I was shocked and hurt that neither of them made a single phone call or email to enquire after my welfare in the days and weeks following this interview, though I was painfully thin and clearly distraught when they saw me.) Martin asked if he could keep my transcript to show the Bishop. I agreed and also gave him an outstanding assignment that I had already completed prior to events kicking off. I got my lowest score for that assignment by a country mile and narrowly avoided failing the module. In the end, it didn't matter anyway.

We were thanked for coming and told to make our own way out. We weren't seen off the premises; Martin and Susannah remained in the boardroom. This made me feel as if I had profoundly shocked and disappointed them, although with hindsight, I expect they had found the interview as difficult as we had. We drove home in stunned silence. I then went to Hillary's for a few hours to 'dry off' before facing the children.

Some days later, I learnt that Penny had also been interviewed, but in her own sitting room with only the Diocesan Safeguarding Officer, Antonia (Toni) King, present. As Toni King was a mutual acquaintance of both Penny and me, this felt highly inappropriate. Whilst not close friends, Toni and I had been out for a curry together earlier that year and I had been due to give her a lift to

Diocesan House that weekend for the Reader training day I was not allowed to attend. Up to that point, we had got on well, enjoying a bit of banter and intellectual sparring.

The anticipated phone call from the Bishop within ten days never came. In fact, it didn't come until over a month later. In this period of not knowing my fate, I was provided with no pastoral support, and relied on prayer, friends and Richard Newborne, my new spiritual director, to get me through. Geraint Boyce was forbidden from engaging at a pastoral level with us, though he rang us regularly to check on my health and was always willing to listen without comment. (He spoke to Ed as I wasn't well enough to take calls.) Though he was not allowed to be partisan in any way, I felt supported and upheld by Geraint in the minimal way he could offer. I could not speak to my usual spiritual director, Ann McVeigh, for reasons of confidentiality because she was linked to St Bart's, plus there was the added complication that her daughter played in the church worship band with Penny. (I was dismayed to hear that Lynda Hope, the church-warden, had been chastised by the Bishop for appearing too close to me. Lynda was the only woman in any form of authority at our church whom I was able to talk to at this time, and I certainly never felt that she compromised her integrity as church-warden in any sense.)

As the weeks rolled on, there was still no word from Bishop Andrew, despite numerous desperate phone calls and emails from myself, Geraint and our youth worker, Jo, who had been incredibly supportive of me. My mental health went into further decline and I lost more weight. I was under the care of my GP for severe depression and a team of friends from church sat with me every morning until the end of June and made me lunch, as I could not be left alone, with Ed at work and the kids at school. It wasn't exactly suicide-watch but there was a clear concern for my welfare. Where possible, Ed rejigged work commitments to work from home to be with me. I cannot begin to convey how amazingly loving, compassionate and supportive he was throughout this terrible time. To this day I remain deeply ashamed of all I put him through.

We could not go to church as a family because Geraint had been expressly told by the Bishop that Penny was *not* to be asked to step down from any of her commitments. This made it impossible for us to worship there as she sang in the worship band and helped out with the youth members. I had to withdraw my elder son from youth group while she was co-leading sessions. Moreover, Dorothy Flint was still on rota for leading services and preaching and I felt deeply betrayed by her as well, justifiably or not.

By the end of May, four weeks since I'd met with Martin and Susannah, I was beside myself with hurt and betrayal. I had learnt that Penny was being her usual exuberant self at church, and still singing in the worship band. It felt so cruel and unfair when we were stuck at home with the kids, coming up with creative excuses for why we weren't going to church and why I wasn't attending my course any more. While I understood the arguments about 'not shooting the messenger', it still felt unjust given our mutual role in events and her apparent lack of remorse, despite the greater responsibility falling on my shoulders.

I regret it now, but I fired off an email to everyone who knew, expressing my sheer and utter agony and dismay that this person who (in my highly subjective view) had tried to sabotage me, my family, my church and my ministry was allowed to joke around at church as if nothing had happened while my life was disintegrating all around me. I purposefully copied it to Toni King, too, as I thought it would reach the Bishop. I also threw in an ungracious comment about the spiritual discernment process. This email was not very savvy of me – it was downright suicidal, to be frank – but I wasn't thinking straight. I was desperate for action and it seemed the only way, as Bishop Andrew was not returning Geraint Boyce's desperate phone calls and emails.

It was effective, anyway, as a few days later I received a phone call from the Bishop, while I was at a friend's house. He started off the phone call much in the manner that Susannah had four weeks ago, stating that no one was judging me and that he spoke to me as a brother in Christ. I appreciated him saying this. I also appreciated how gracious he was when my mobile connection kept cracking up. He phoned back numerous times until we resorted to my friend's landline!

He would not say a bad word against Penny but acknowledged my sense of hurt and betrayal. I found the way he oscillated between kindliness and anger difficult to deal with. I was criticised for telling so many people about what had happened; I defended myself by saying I would have told a great deal fewer people had it not dragged on for so long, but I felt he was cross with me for my indiscretion and I guess, for 'dumping him in it'. He then outlined a proposal for me but, before I had responded, said it wasn't really a proposal, he was insisting on it.

The Bishop then outlined that there were three options – time out for a year but resume Reader training and be licensed to St Bart's at the end of it; time out for a year but resume Reader training and be licensed elsewhere; be deemed unsuitable for public ministry and part ways with the Diocese. He made it clear that any of these three outcomes were a possibility.

A meeting with me and Ed was then arranged for that evening at Bishop's House. He stated that Toni King would be there, too, in her capacity as Diocesan Safeguarding Officer. My heart sank. This did not feel appropriate, given her social links to Penny and me, but I felt I would do myself no favours by complaining.

When we got there, the Bishop was exceedingly friendly and gracious. Toni got up and held her arms out to hug me (in her capacity as friend or Safeguarding Officer? I wasn't sure), but I felt this was inappropriate and held back (indeed, I felt that the whole issue of crossing boundaries was far from restricted to my behaviour throughout this painful process). I remember that Toni had a large ring-binder of notes on her lap and was clearly taking notes again that evening. I found the ring-binder off-putting; it made me feel as if I had done something really dreadful to necessitate so many notes (though of course, in reality, it was probably just a general work folder).

The Bishop opened in prayer and reiterated that no one was judging me. He was appreciative of Ed's presence and the atmosphere felt initially convivial. He repeated his 'proposal'. Ed queried, as Geraint Boyce and others would do subsequently, what on earth I was supposed to do with my time for a whole year. The whole structure of my week would be gone, without Reader training and participation in service leading. The Bishop spoke of a 'provision' he would make for me, involving seeing a pastoral assistant of his choice, and possibly accessing a diocesan-approved counsellor if that felt helpful. This was fine, but I couldn't see how it would go any way to filling my days. He spoke several times of addressing two main issues – processing my sense of hurt and betrayal via counselling or pastoral support (with a view to a reconciliation of sorts with Penny), and working on my boundaries. I fully acknowledged then, as I do now, that I stepped over a boundary in my role as leader and that of course that needed addressing.

Things turned rather heated as Ed enquired why the Bishop had taken so long to reach a decision, leaving me in a bad way and us in a desperate place as a family. The Bishop defended himself using the spiritual discernment argument, but Ed was not having any of it, citing the example of the corporate world, where you would at least send out a 'we're dealing with it' letter to reassure the person concerned. The Bishop said spiritual discernment was very different from the corporate world and Ed replied that indeed it was, but, if anything, the Church should be more compassionate and communicative than a commercial organisation, rather than less so. Ed held his ground and the Bishop conceded that he had made errors of communication and apologised graciously. We appreciated that.

Toni reassured us that during her interview with Penny, Penny had admitted that I hadn't coerced her into any physical activity and that the kiss had been mutual. Ed and I both queried the congruence of her allegation, if I hadn't made unwelcome physical advances and it was mutual. Toni said her allegation was congruent, but wouldn't say why. Again, we were not allowed to hear what Penny had said about me. But again, admittedly, I didn't really want to know the full extent of it, because I felt I had to protect my mental health for the good of myself and my family. I was very fragile at that time. Toni spoke of the many awful cases she had had to deal with in her role in the Diocese. Ed asked her why they were making such a big fuss about this, if she was so busy with big clergy issues, but she didn't answer. I insisted that nothing was put in writing about me concerning 'sexual advances' because it was a lie and made me sound like some kind of sexual predator. The Bishop reassured me that nothing would be put in writing that suggested I had forced myself physically on Penny in any way.

There then followed a discussion about my theology. This appeared to be as problematic as my dalliance with Penny. The Bishop accused me in so many words of indoctrinating Penny with liberal theology concerning the Bible and homosexuality. I defended myself by saying this was in response to homophobic remarks and YouTube clips of reparative therapy she had sent me, which I had found deeply upsetting, not to mention ironic in the circumstances. He advised me to keep my personal views on this subject to myself and not to express them in public. I also registered my concerns at the Flints' role in all of this, which I found astounding given their age, experience and senior roles in the church leadership team. The Bishop, understandably and appropriately, wasn't going to comment on his own clergy.

The Bishop summed up by saying that I needed to 'learn to manage my sexuality'. This statement bemused and bothered me, and has done ever since. Was it a homophobic remark? Would he have said that to someone who had engaged in a 'straight' kiss?

I was told that the Bishop would be in touch with regards to my pastoral 'provision' and he wished us a good holiday, as we were off to France early the next morning. He saw us to the door and was friendly and gracious. Nevertheless, I came home feeling upset and angry. Although I fully accepted that I had behaved entirely inappropriately, I felt that I had been judged on the basis of dubious allegations made about me. I was made to feel that I had proselytised Penny and was some kind of low-level sex offender. I did not recognise this version of me. These may seem quite harsh words now, and on reflection a bit OTT, but it's how I felt at the time. Again the Bishop displayed a confusing mixture of anger and kindness, but while I felt angry with his attitude towards me at points, he was a great deal friendlier and more gracious than Canon Martin Langley had been at Diocesan House and I felt warmth towards him despite my frustration and stress. In some ways, I'd like to dislike him, because of how I was treated, but I don't.

On Sunday 12 June, Bishop Andrew covered my preaching slot at St Bart's. I wasn't there, but apparently his sermon was about forgiveness and was deemed compassionate and highly apt. That afternoon he had a long meeting with Geraint and Fred, the male church-warden, about the situation. This was the first time, as far as I can gather, that he actually consulted anyone about my character and abilities. I was relieved this meeting was finally taking place, as I felt confident Fred and Geraint would give a good account of me. I have never claimed to be wise, but I have always prided myself on my honesty and integrity and I hoped and prayed they would do me proud.

In the evening, the Bishop rang me. He was a great deal friendlier and said that Geraint had spoken highly of my competency and popularity at St Bart's. Geraint had told him that my teaching was important and meant a lot to people and that I was extremely gifted. The Bishop told me it was now the least likely scenario that I would be asked to leave my training. I felt reassured by this, as well as by his friendlier tone. He also released me to speak to Geraint Boyce in a pastoral capacity again. Over the course of the next few weeks, I began to regain some mental and physical strength, though I was not attending church due to Penny's continued presence there.

Just as I was beginning to feel more positive, I received a phone call from Geraint Boyce on 3 July. He told me that a number of people on the existing and past PCC had received an anonymous letter through the post. He indicated that it was extremely unpleasant but wouldn't go into details on the phone. He said he had scanned it and emailed it to me but that I should wait until Ed was to read it. So I knew it was going to be bad.

I had to carry on cooking dinner and dealing with the children with my heart thumping and my stomach lurching, knowing that a pdf-nasty was waiting for me upstairs on the PC. When Ed got back, we disappeared upstairs and opened the document. It was a vile and salacious anonymous letter, poorly punctuated, with a damning critique of Roy's leadership. But the bulk of the letter focused on me and Penny, accusing me of sexually abusing a member of the congregation and twisting Scripture to justify my sexuality. It also accused my husband of supporting 'three in a marriage'. It lambasted the wardens and youth workers for siding with me in this cover-up of sexual abuse, and Geraint of kowtowing to the Bishop in 'whitewashing' the whole affair. As the stuff contained within it was entirely partisan, totally on Penny's side with no mention of the Revd Robert Flint and his wife, I could only assume it came either from Penny herself, or someone she had confided in. The thought that someone within our congregation had possibly sent it caused me enormous pain.

There was a heated phone call between Ed and Geraint in which Geraint refused to let Ed attend the emergency PCC meeting to be held that evening. Ed had insisted everyone sign a confidentiality agreement as one or two of the biggest church gossips were on the PCC, but Geraint felt that he couldn't organise that in time, or indeed wondered if it was lawful to do so. Penny had also asked to come when Geraint had rung her. She had claimed to know nothing about the letter and denied ever saying I had sexually abused her and was willing to say as much to the PCC. To avoid a 'kangaroo court' scenario, Geraint refused to let either Ed or Penny attend. I was hysterical, yelling and screaming in the background as Ed spoke to him on the phone and later, when Fred the warden rang, concerned for our welfare.

Later on that evening, I received a number of texts from friends on the PCC. There had been unilateral support for Ed and me. Geraint had made it abundantly clear that whilst an allegation had been made, there was categorically no issue of sexual abuse. Apparently there had been a massive sense of unity and support for us as a family and that meant a tremendous amount to me.

Bishop Andrew also emailed in encouragement and support. In this email, he also outlined in writing for the first time the twofold areas I needed to work on, as per the chat at Bishop's House. The next day, one of the youth leaders texted me to say that Penny had left St Bart's and was going to the Victory Church, a large free evangelical church nearby. I wondered what impact the letter and the church reaction to the letter had had on this decision.

Toni King then asked to meet me for coffee, which I agreed to, though I was unsure in what capacity she meant. As I was still in shock from the anonymous letter, I asked if she could meet me at home as I didn't feel well enough to go out in public. It transpired her call was not social, but at the behest of the Bishop. Apparently she had been charged with meeting me every three to four weeks to check that I was unlikely to do anything to harm myself or the Church. I wondered if she would have explained this had I not asked the purpose of her call. Again, that sense of boundary crossing was an issue. It was not made clear in her email that this was anything other than a social chat. Once I knew this, I wished I had not asked her to the house, as it felt as if this was an intrusion on my home life. I already felt my front room was 'tainted' from the meeting with Geraint on 26 April when he read out the charges.

This meeting made me feel anxious and irritated and it felt strange seeing Toni in this capacity. I was cross because she seemed insensitive to the needs of my children. I kept saying that the children would be home soon and we were off camping straight from school, but she didn't seem to take the hint. When my elder son returned home from secondary school, Toni made an offhand comment to him. Carter is more than capable of holding his own, but it was symptomatic of the boundary-crossing behaviour that was a common thread throughout this process.

I had to more or less turf her out in the end. There was no hug goodbye, though she seemed to be expecting it, and I told her I couldn't see her socially if I had to see her in this capacity. I felt as if it was left to me to address the boundary between us, as she made it clear she was quite happy to have these chats over a coffee or a curry at the weekend. On the following Monday, I emailed the

Bishop and asked if I could see somebody else for these meetings, as I felt there was a clear boundary issue. He didn't reply.

When Toni contacted me again to meet up at the end of July, I wasn't sure whether Bishop Andrew had read my email but chosen to ignore it, or just hadn't read it. I wasn't sure what to do in my best interests, as I didn't want to be seen as awkward, so I agreed to a further meeting with Toni. This time, I chose a large garden centre that was relatively anonymous to meet. This meeting was far more positive. Toni seemed very supportive of me, saying it would be a crime if someone with my skill-set and talents wasn't allowed to progress. We engaged in theological debate on issues concerning sexuality. I had noted on many occasions that, for someone who claimed to be so against homosexual behaviour, she seemed to bring up the subject an awful lot. Clearly it was not a problem for *her* to discuss homosexuality, even if I was banned from doing so.

Later that summer, I learnt that the Victory Church had contacted Geraint Boyce to request a reconciliatory meeting between Penny and myself prior to the school holidays. I had refused to do this, as I was still very unwell and didn't want my mental health to further decline when I had three children at home for six weeks. Victory asked again at the end of August. I had just come back from a family holiday in France, and resented being asked to confront the Penny issue so soon after, but gathered Victory had been putting pressure on Geraint to arrange a meeting between Penny and myself. So Geraint then arranged a meeting with me to chat about this, to which Hillary Norris was also invited as my support.

I felt tense and teary. Geraint, as ever, was intelligent and sensitive. I discussed my fears around Penny coming to a meeting 'unrepentant', thereby making reconciliation impossible. We talked a great deal about forgiveness, especially of the one-way variety, and of the pros and cons

of holding a meeting. It was difficult, and I felt under a great
deal of stress, but I felt supported by Geraint and Hillary.
Both of them made it clear that Penny's view that I was a
danger to women was her view only; nobody else shared
that view of me. I expressed my anger and frustration that
whilst I had conceded a great deal of ground and admitted
to some pretty excruciating behaviour on my part, she had
kept totally silent about her sexuality and her expressions
of physical desire for me.

We were just drawing to a close when our prayers
were punctuated by loud music and singing. I realised to
my abject horror (and Geraint and Hillary's) that it was
Thursday evening, and therefore the worship band that
Penny was still part of were rehearsing downstairs in the
worship area. Geraint ran out to check whether it was
Penny singing. It was.

I became very distraught and started crying
hysterically. Hillary smuggled me out of the building while
Geraint distracted the band. I sat in Hillary's car for some
time with her in order to calm down, before driving home
myself. My reaction to Penny's presence in the building
served as proof to them that I was not ready for a meeting
with her and not ready to forgive at that point.

One thing I do remember clearly from that torturous
evening was this – Hillary holding my hand and telling
me, 'Jaime, when you've got over this – and you will –
you're going to be amazing.' I nodded. Somehow, amid
the copious mounds of steaming shit that had hit the fan,
I believed that. I really did.

On 11 September, I had my first meeting with the
Revd Canon Olivia Fenton-Hayes, the pastoral assistant
assigned to me by Bishop Andrew. Olivia allowed me to
tell the story in my own words, asking for clarification on
certain points. I felt listened to, supported and upheld in
prayer. I didn't feel that I was fighting against someone
else's preconceptions or theology and felt respected
intellectually for the first time. Olivia later emailed

A Living Nightmare

Bishop Andrew, copying me in, to say there was nothing in either my demeanour or my story to cause her to doubt that I was telling anything other than the truth. I'd been an idiot, let my feelings run away with me and behaved entirely inappropriately for someone in my position, but that was all. I was no dangerous sexual predator; no daughters required locking up.

A week later, several people from church received an emotional and lengthy email from Robert and Dorothy Flint, Penny's supporters, informing us that they were leaving the church due to theological differences. (I later found out that there had been a heated argument between themselves and the church leadership over their fundamentalist views on homosexuality.) Ed and I received a slightly tailored version, in which they expressed sympathy with all that we must have gone through. This felt (at best) incredibly odd, given their role in the affair. I adjudged the email to the church to be indiscreet and ill-advised, and for me, did not speak of love for St Bart's. But I was also only too aware that when we are hurting, it is hard to consider the bigger picture of our actions. So I replied after a week or so, expressing my regret at the manner of their leaving and making it clear that I bore them no ill-will. (I believe they acted from sincerely held beliefs, beliefs held by many evangelical Christians of their generation. They are not my views, but they are not untypical of many people in their sixties and seventies inside and outside of churches around the country.)

Another 'catch-up' was organised for the following week between Toni King and me, this time at a café bar in the town centre. This went pretty much as previous meetings, with me feeling that I was chatting to a mate, but wondering at the same time whether I should be watching what I said a bit more and what was getting fed back to the Bishop. I feel embarrassed by flippant comments I made during these conversations, but it was hard for me, because I knew Toni as a humorous, witty woman in a personal capacity and as an equal. So it was difficult to switch modes. I felt irritated that Toni felt the need to constantly say 'you know my theology', as if to constantly underline that she felt differently from me about sexuality issues. This statement gave me the impression that she felt I was 'wrong'. It didn't feel helpful to have a self-confessed conservative evangelical as my link person with the Bishop. It felt that I was always at a disadvantage. In addition, the way that the same diocesan people seem to perform multiple roles may have been a logistical and financial necessity, but it created for me a sense of 'in-house chumminess' (for example, Toni referred to the area dean, Nigel Higgs, as 'Higgsy'). Such incestuous working relationships worked against me, by denying me an impartial and professional service. I suspect their response to that would have been, you've not behaved in an impartial and professional way towards a congregant as a trainee church leader, which would be true, but somewhat beside the point.

Just as it was nearly time to close, as I had to be back for the school run, Toni dropped what felt like a bombshell to me. She asked me what the Bishop had told me he required of me. I repeated the twofold areas of addressing my boundary issues and processing my hurt and betrayal. She asked if I had talked to him recently. I said I had seen him at St Bart's on 9 September and that he had reiterated the same two areas. She frowned and stuttered around for a while as if hiding something, then said she felt there were other areas 'lurking around' that he was expecting me to deal with. I looked shocked. Whilst I appreciated the information, it upset me and worried me that there were areas of concern that I had not been informed of. This seemed grossly unfair to me and I said as much. Toni agreed and said that she would badger the Bishop to put down his requirements in writing for me. I was left feeling confused, disillusioned and upset, and nearly drove into the back of someone on the way home as the tears streamed down my face. Hurrah for ABS.

I was very distraught all weekend, feeling that nothing was going to be good enough. I had the sense that they didn't really want me as a Reader and that they saw me as a liability – that they were going to make me jump through an endless series of hoops in the hope I would eventually just slink off into the sunset. I had been reading voraciously since my removal from Reader training, and a quote from *People of Passion: What the Churches Teach about Sex* was haunting me:

> Bisexuality … is the church's deepest sexual fear … for bisexuals undermine the whole sexual system, the neat classification of people into homosexual and heterosexual, the pathologizing of homosexuality as a heterosexual disorder and so on. Bisexuality represents desire unfettered, and perhaps that is why those who experience it are so studiously unacknowledged in church documents, and on the odd occasion where they are acknowledged they are pathetically misrepresented as sexual indiscriminate and promiscuous.[1]

I cried a lot and didn't sleep most of the weekend. By Monday morning, I had rubbed my eyes so much, my eyelids had turned purple, as if I had a black eye. I emailed the Bishop and outlined my concerns at not knowing exactly what was required of me. He didn't reply.

A few weeks later, I was prescribed a higher dose of antidepressants, as the current dosage of 50mg was barely touching the sides. I was also prescribed the sleeping drug Zoplicone, following two weeks of near sleepless nights. The past few weeks had been like wading through

---

[1] Elizabeth Stuart and Adrian Thatcher, *People of Passion: What the Churches Teach about Sex* (Burns & Oates,1997).

treacle, just trying to carry out basic functions. If I had to highlight one part of the process that had felt most damaging, it would have been the timescales involved. I don't think the powers that be realise that when you're in the throes of depression, a day feels like a week and a week like a month. When you can't sleep at night due to anxiety, stress and shame, the long-drawn-out process of spiritual discernment feels like an unnecessary and cruel torture. I have photographs of a family trip to Legoland that month where my face is drawn and pinched and my clothes are hanging off me, with a bad case of 'old lady bottom' going on in my jeans.

Most of the events above formed the basis of a reflection I sent to Canon Olivia in October 2012. Olivia thanked me for the 'very open and moving account of the nightmare you have been living through'.

One of the great ironies of the horrible events of spring 2012 was that I was on the cusp of taking a module on Christian ethics prior to my enforced withdrawal from Reader training. This module covered natural law and sexuality issues. I suspect the Diocese had no desire to see me spread my liberal views further afield.

The months that followed continued to be very distressing for me. On the grapevine, I heard that Penny was now well ensconced at the Victory Church and was even recording a worship album (though not under their patronage). This just twisted the knife even deeper as I continued to stagger through each day in a tear-stained, drugged-up fug of shame and anger. I vacillated backwards and forwards with the decision of whether to agree to a meeting with her or not, but in the end, I just couldn't see how it would achieve anything but send me even closer to the edge. Mutual acquaintances told me there wasn't a trace of remorse in her heart, so what was the point? I had already conceded a great deal of ground through my natural propensity towards auto-download and self-flagellation; it was time she dismounted her horse at high altitude. There was stalemate, which pleased neither church in the equation.

Finally, following a plea on my behalf from Canon Olivia, I heard word from the Bishop. I had requested that I should *not* see Toni King any more, as I was finding her unhelpful to say the least. Amongst other things, Bishop Andrew suggested I prayed, 'Lord: what is it Toni is saving me from?'

Was this a threat of imminent ex-communication or just plain homophobia? Olivia wasn't sure either. She had long since explained to me that despite my insistence that the whole fleeting episode with Penny had been more Radio 4 than Channel 4, the Diocese would have it firmly filed under SEX. I was de facto a sex offender, as far as they were concerned. Olivia had also made it clear that I could wave goodbye to any future aspirations involving the 'O' word, as a kiss was deemed a sexual act and homosexual acts were not permitted among ordained or lay ministers in the Church of England. In that sense, I may as well have spent the night in a hotel room with her for all the difference it made. Whilst my infidelity to Ed and my abuse of a church leadership position were certainly key issues, it was undoubtedly the (homo) sexual aspect of what had happened that was influencing their decision-making (or lack of), in Olivia's view.

Another incident that hurt me deeply around that time was the behaviour of the Vicar of St Bart's. Though he had stepped down temporarily on health grounds, Roy Littlecombe was still very much on the scene with his wife and extended family. Long before the episode with Penny had kicked off, I had promised to take his family to the airport so that they didn't have to order a second taxi or pay expensive airport parking fees en route to their holiday apartment.

When the time came, after the whole thing with Penny had blown up, Denise Littlecombe texted me twice to say there was no need, they would just order another taxi. Being the naïve muppet that I am, always believing the best in people, I thought they were just trying to avoid putting me to any trouble. Denise then relented and told me to come a little earlier and share a coffee. When I got there, she explained that Roy had already gone ahead with their two daughters and the grandchildren and that I was only taking Denise and their two sons-in-law to the airport. She then took me out into the garden for a coffee, which she had never done before. It was a sunny autumnal day, though not particularly hot.

Denise was someone with whom I had always got on fantastically well and I had always felt at ease talking to her. But my 'sin' had interrupted the easy flow of conversation between us. I spoke of the injustice I felt; she spoke of the sin I had committed, in a gently patronising tone but with a kindly look in her eyes. I found that quite difficult to process. Sometime later, the two sons-in-law appeared. Suddenly the phone rang. Denise answered it. It was Roy checking that she had remembered to unload the dishwasher. Or so I naïvely believed, until it sunk in later – who on earth rings their partner to check they've unloaded the clean dishes from the dishwasher before going on holiday? When we eventually arrived at the airport, I said to Denise as we unloaded the boot, 'I do know I stuffed up', as she seemed to feel I was unrepentant. (I have no idea where she got that idea; I was beside myself with anger and despair but had more than acknowledged my culpability – clearly that had not come across.) She replied with more than a degree of condescension, 'Well, that's one thing, at least.' I got in the car and drove off. I did not look back.

Whenever I encountered conservative evangelical

acquaintances from that time, I would smile benignly – but in my head I would be thinking, 'You have no idea how my life is, what it is to exist outside of your boy-meets-girl 4.8 grandchildren existence. You have no concept of the pain I have gone through and how long it has taken to piece my broken life back together into some semblance of normality.' It strikes me now, as it struck me then, just how ignorant so many self-identified Christians are of the reality and messiness of same-sex attraction as experienced by those who have to live with it/support it on a daily basis. I guess in the eyes of many evangelical Christians, I am an adulteress, in spirit if not necessarily in body. Well, maybe I am according to their interpretation of Scripture, but I'd just like these 'Bible-based' Christians to consider for one moment how it feels to need closeness with both men and women to feel mentally whole, to function in daily life, to love my husband and bring up my children. I am damned if I do; damned if I don't. I ignore my need for same-sex affection at my mental peril, with the associated impact on my family; I risk the wrath of the Conservative Right if I 'give in' to it by hugging a woman for longer than thirty seconds. In this particular instance, I made a huge error of judgement, but to adhere to the Church of England's advice to exclusively follow my heterophile leanings would ironically lead to the very personality disorder the C of E claims I already have.

It's not ignorance so much that hurts, it's *proactive* ignorance. It's that complete antipathy, even distaste, towards even considering that some people just cannot, through no fault of their own, fit the heterosexual, monosexual mould. It shocks me that for all the evidence to the contrary, so many Christians still believe God made a heterosexual world where men and women fall in love and create an exclusive family unit, with anything outside of this a mistake to be rectified. Surely the very figure of

Jesus Christ, who gravitated towards the marginalised and the cast out, challenges such notions?

The old adage, that you know who your friends are when the chips are down, was certainly true in this period of my life. Some church members went over and above the call of duty, particularly the youth and children's workers, Jo, Eloise and Charlesy, the wardens Fred and Lynda, and my good friends Celine, Hillary and Nadine. Others were more circumspect. For some years, I had been very friendly with a spiritual director who occasionally attended St Bart's, Ann McVeigh. As I explored ministry, she became my own SD, even though it wasn't strictly ethical, since she was a member of the same church. But she had always been incredibly supportive of both me as a person, and of my preaching ministry, so it just felt like the obvious choice. She was someone whose input in my life I truly valued.

As the discussion went round and round of whether I should agree to a 'reconciliation' meeting with Penny, I naturally asked Ann if she would accompany me to this, if indeed I followed through with it. She was the obvious choice, having been at my side in conversation and prayer throughout much of the saga. I was stunned when her reply was 'No. I'd rather stay independent of the process.' I understood her allegiance to her patrons at the Diocese, who promoted her ministry, but this felt like a punch to the stomach at the time. I felt hurt and disillusioned and there was an almighty *clank* as she toppled off the pedestal I'd put her on. Of course, with the benefit of polished glasses, I now see that I placed her in a horrendous position and perhaps it was naïve of me to have expected anything else, given the patronage her ministry received from the Diocese. Ann was a great support to me for a long period of my time at St Bart's, as was her gloriously eccentric husband, and whilst I have no desire to step back into that world, I know the door would be open.

A desperate Midnight Mass service at St Bart's prefaced a miserable Christmas, where the whole family came down with the norovirus and all of our visitors cancelled on us. My elder son was so sick we had to remove the pipes from the bathroom sink to unblock them. I left that particularly lovely job to Ed!

I think Christmas Eve 2012 probably marked the start of my realisation that the preaching dream was over, and that it was maybe time to walk another street.[2] I sat anonymously in the back row and cried most of the way through the beautiful candlelit service led by the Archdeacon. A woman at church whom I'd never had much time for turned around and gave me a big long hug. That meant a lot. It was never the people, for the most part, that drove our decision to leave St Bart's. The majority of those responsible for the nasty stuff had felt the wrath of Geraint and the wardens' tongues and had now left. It was the bureaucracy and hypocrisy of the Church hierarchy that stank. I remained fantastically supported by the wardens – Fred and Lynda, Fred's wife Nadine, Hillary Norris and the Revd Geraint Boyce. The youth workers at St Bart's, Jo and Eloise, were also incredibly loyal to me and fully shared my inclusive views on sexuality. Eloise remains a close friend, one of the only survivors of my time there. St Bart's was and is a great church. The structure that supports it is not.

Weirdly, a favourite ornament of mine cracked into pieces that Christmas – a candleholder in the shape of a church that glowed inside when you lit a tea light in it. I guess the flame got too hot because the church suddenly

---

[2] Again, a reference to Portia Nelson's poem, freely available on the Web.

cracked and the roof fell in. I glued it back together, but it was never the same again. I've kept it, as some kind of sad reminder of a broken dream, but it's not on the mantelpiece at Christmas any more.

In the end, it took until February 2013 for Ed and me to wake up and smell the coffee, an entirely apt metaphor for two Starbucks aficionados! We had been dipping in and out of a local free church for a few months and had made a few friends there (see next chapter), and although we were by no means sure that this new place was right for us, we knew we couldn't stay at St Bart's. For one thing, the children were unaware of the actual allegations made against me, but the presence of that evil anonymous letter meant that the whole family was incredibly vulnerable to vicious rumours. It was in the interests of the whole family, but especially the children, to remove them from potential sources of gossip as far as we could. I continued to have many sleepless nights about them finding out at school from another church kid and their whole education subsequently being ruined, but at least they were out of the main firing line.

Prior to informing the Bishop of our decision, I thought it only fair to let Geraint Boyce know. I hesitated slightly, as Geraint himself had terrible stuff going on at home, but in the end I knew I owed it to him to find out first, as he had been so supportive of me, despite maintaining the necessary neutrality when required.

We met in a garden centre not too close to home and found a seat away from the noisy gaggles of pensioners who frequent such places, (I now avoid garden centres like the plague, as they always remind me of my year of hell, since so many conversations of note took place in them.) I told him of my decision and at my absolute incandescence at what had transpired. I know that he had been mightily challenged over LGBT issues by the whole affair and stunned at some of the homophobic views espoused by many of the individuals at the heart of the episode. I had given him much food for thought. He was very upset that we had decided to leave St Bart's and hadn't seen it coming at all. He genuinely thought I had only met with him to tell him I was leaving Reader training, not leaving the Church of England and St Bart's full stop. As we said goodbye in the car park, his eyes filled up with tears. He told me I was 'special', then turned to go back to his car.

Ed composed a letter on our behalf to Bishop Andrew on Valentine's Day 2013, though we signed it from Ed only, as the Bishop had stated on a number of occasions that he deemed Ed to be 'a remarkable man'. We felt it carried more gravitas coming from Ed, whom he liked and respected, and also, naturally, because he was male. Ed is also far posher than me, which seemed to carry additional weight. Ed wrote some truly wonderful things about me and our marriage in this letter, which meant the absolute world to me. But the main thrust of his letter concerned the disgraceful way in which we were treated as a family by the Church and the Church's continued stance towards LGBT people. I then proceeded to write letters to my tutors and colleagues, as well as to my closest friends, outlining our reasons for leaving the Church of England after fifteen years of service.

Canon Olivia was extremely disappointed, though understanding, to hear of our decision to leave the C of E. She felt I had let the Bishop off lightly, and that he must have been mightily relieved that he no longer had to make a decision over me. I got the impression from her that the Diocese knew they had handled this badly and had treated us pretty appallingly.

In response to these letters, we received a number of supportive emails. A (straight) priestly friend from outside the parish commented that there were 'many within the C of E who share your frustration' and spoke of the painful journey ahead as the Church sought solutions to the sexuality issue. A (straight) course tutor and fellow Reader expressed 'anger at the situation you have been brave enough to leave', and added, 'I respect and share your feelings and convictions entirely'. The tutor in question lamented their own lack of courage in remaining within the Church of England. Another course tutor expressed anger at what had happened to me and denied any involvement in my removal from Reader training.

A senior Anglican clergyman, straight and from another parish, simply replied: 'Thank you … honest, moving and courageous.' The Archdeacon wrote that it was 'saddening to hear how bruised the situation has left you', whilst another (non-Anglican) church pastor commented: 'I can only begin to imagine the sense of turmoil you and Ed must have gone through … it is enough to make me weep.'

The responses from my Reader training colleagues, to whom I'd already confessed the whole sorry affair, perhaps meant the most. One wrote: 'Thank you for your honesty throughout, your integrity, your intellect, your sense of fun … the noise and laughter level has subsided at residentials without you there and I particularly miss your intellect and wit.' Another commented that I had 'so much to offer' and hoped I found a niche for my gifts. I was advised by one colleague to 'lay the anger aside at Jesus' feet; he was rejected by the home team, too, but took a different path.'

A family friend in the USA expressed excitement at our decision alongside sadness: 'There are no limits as to what you can achieve and how many lives you can touch so I hope that you find the strength and courage to use your insight to its full potential.'

A church friend from St Bart's described my letter as 'beautifully and positively written and very moving' yet also 'saddening in the light it casts onto the Church of England, as so many of us cannot support what feels like the exclusivity and rejection demonstrated by the leadership towards Christians who do not fit their very narrow and historically driven categories. Please be assured that hierarchy's views are not shared by many of us ordinary Anglicans.' This friend concluded on a positive note: 'I am sure God has great plans for you, and it will be an amazing and important journey, fruitful for many'.

Altogether less positive, was the reaction of the St Bart's PCC[3] to our leaving. I was in the throes of putting a research proposal together for my doctorate, and had been reading various faith/sexuality publications, including the now notorious *Issues in Human Sexuality* published by the Anglican House of Bishops in 1991. This document contains seventeen pages on 'The Phenomenon of Homosexual Love' yet just ten lines (or 119 words) on bisexuality. Well, St Bart's PCC summed up fifteen years of service to the Church of England in just a short couple of paragraphs, too, with no gratitude for the many, many hours of voluntary service we had both given to the Church. Whilst I gather this letter of March 2013 was in all probability more or less dictated to the wardens by the Diocese, it still felt like a massive kick in the teeth for all that we had given over the years. I had supplied the wardens with my own goodbye letter, but they had clearly been forbidden from reading it out, though I felt it was gracious and balanced. I gather that there was a stunned silence when the actual statement was read out by the PCC, and that the next agenda item was swiftly taken up.

I was told of this announcement some weeks after the event; clearly they were afraid I would 'interlope' in some capacity, had I known in advance that I would not be allowed to say goodbye in my own words. It was obvious I was seen to be a threat, which I took as a compliment and sign of both my perceived popularity and intellectual qualities, as well as a blatant sign of homophobia.

We finally received an acknowledgement from Bishop

---

[3] Parochial Church Council.

Andrew in April, though I did not receive even a courtesy letter from Canon Martin Langley or the Revd Susannah Fulwell, whom I understand are no longer in post. It would not be appropriate to reproduce the Bishop's letter verbatim, but I can tell you that it contained an unreserved apology for not responding sooner to Ed's letter. He spoke of his total respect for our decision to leave the Church of England and commented that 'the C of E is the poorer for your departure'. He continued by stating that he believed us to be 'Christian people of integrity' and spoke of our 'deeply held commitments and convictions'. He made it clear that he understood and respected the rationale for our leaving and that he was always available to us, at his place or ours.

Such a letter, containing as it did both a real apology and a veiled apology, meant a great deal to Ed and me, enabling us to attain a certain amount of closure and a 'good ending' to life in the Church of England, if not at St Bart's. We were both very impressed with the genuine and heartfelt sentiments expressed within it, as well as the generosity of spirit that accompanied it. At various points in the whole episode, I had been unsure of whether I liked Bishop Andrew or not. On reflection I did. It was the system he was bound to operate within that stank to high heaven.

It was with this letter safely filed away at home that I now felt able to countenance taking part in a formal confession exercise with Canon Olivia. She had suggested it somewhere along the line, but I had not felt ready for it. However, the time felt ripe, though I would only consider doing this with Olivia, who had loyally stood by me throughout the process, believing in my honesty and integrity, two values that are core to my very being.

As preparation for this, I was required to read a few books and follow the reflective spiritual exercises therein. I was then to compose a formal confession to be read out in the chapel at the Cathedral before God and

A Living Nightmare

Olivia. This duly took place one sunny day in June 2013. I have not reproduced this document, as its contents are between me and God, but I do look back on it and think I was still in the throes of fundamentalist thought! All the same, God knows my heart and which bits were truly me, and which bits were the me I thought I ought to be.

Naturally I confessed my infidelity and my abuse of power. But part of my confession involved an admission that I had dabbled in astrology during my *anus horribilis*. Some measure of regression to my pre-Christian me had seen me apply for a personal chart from 'top' astrologer, Jonathan Cainer, using a pen-name. It came back frighteningly accurate. It didn't feel generic at all, which is the frequent criticism levied at astrological charts, but scarily descriptive of the sort of person I am. I am a bit of a showman, who needs to entertain and be admired, an egotist who throws herself creatively into one project after another. Sometimes that project is a person; fortunately, I do have someone safe and forgiving in the background to mop up the havoc wreaked by my sensual excesses.

What can I say? It had the less nice version of me down to a tee. I'm not sure where this quirky little detour figured on the journey to self-discovery, but it did give me a bit of a jolt, as well as a nervous giggle. I never told Ed about that little episode – far too embarrassed!

I also got into the Enneagram Personality Type Indicator during my year out of church. Based on Jungian psychology, this is altogether more helpful as a method of understanding your strengths and weaknesses, especially in relation to others around you, and is sometimes used by spiritual advisors, too. I came out as a One (there are nine types, as the name 'enneagram' suggests), so I am your classic leader with the propensity to let self-criticism and perfectionist tendencies hold them back. Other Ones include Hillary Clinton, Joan of Arc and Mahatma Gandhi, so I was in revered company!

After the confessional deed was done, Olivia bought me a coffee at the Cathedral. She bumped into several acquaintances and I felt proud when she introduced me as her friend, Jaime. She then told me something interesting, as we made our way across the cathedral green afterwards: she had bumped into Bishop Andrew at a formal service recently. Olivia had told him that she was meeting up with me to lead me in formal confession and he had looked pleased. She had then informed him that he had a made a grave mistake, allowing me to leave the Church of England. Apparently he didn't say anything.

The Revd Richard Coles perhaps sums up my feelings about this episode better than I ever could:

> *I love the Church of England. But it is not wise to love organisations because they do not love you back. They do what organisations do, sometimes close ranks, lie, betray, disappoint, take you out at dawn and shoot you.*[4]

[4] Richard Coles, *Fathomless Riches, Or How I Went from Pop to Pulpit*, London: Weidenfeld & Nicholson, 2014

9

Another Street

2013–2015

Conversion means going out of oneself, being open to God and others; it implies a break, but above all, it means following a new path. For that very reason, it is not an inward-looking, private attitude, but a process which occurs in the socio-economic, political and cultural medium in which life goes on, and which is to be transformed.

Ernesto Cardenal[1]

Whilst the conciliatory and complimentary letter from the Bishop helped me attain a significant degree of closure, I cannot deny that it felt like a form of bereavement, leaving behind my vocation and friends at St Bart's. Church involvement of one variety or another had been part of my daily existence for the past twenty-five years, and St Bart's part of it for the last eleven. I had many close friends there, but while I tried to stay in touch with some of them following our letter of resignation, it was just too difficult. They would inevitably talk about people and events related to St

[1] Preface to *Practical Theology of Liberation*, Hugo Assmann, 1975 (Search Press, UK).

Bart's, which just opened up the barely healed wound time and time again. I hope they forgive me, but for my own mental health, I just had to leave that world behind totally. It's not my style to cut off those who have been loyal to me, but in this instance I needed to get well for the sake of Ed and the children. One year of my life had already been flushed down the pan by this whole painful episode; I didn't want to spend any more time in that hole in the ground.

The main exception to this rule was Celine. She got the whole issue around moving on and I felt I could spend time with her and speak about life outside of church. It helped that we share the same liberal theology and have a similar taste in music, with some notable exceptions which I won't disclose for fear of embarrassing her. Another great thing about Celine is that she doesn't need to talk the whole time, unlike many women. She can cope with silence, so if I wasn't feeling too great, we could go out for a walk without me feeling I needed to talk. That was a valuable quality.

You will guess by my use of the present tense that Celine and I are still very much the best of friends. We have got closer and closer and she has, over the past couple of years, largely filled that yawning gap in my life. I don't personally believe that any one person can completely fill the hole. And I certainly don't subscribe to the notion of a God-shaped hole and other classics from the Evangelical Cheese Emporium. Whilst I feel God's presence all around me, I can't see how a spiritual being can fill a physical ache to be held, to laugh and have fun. Jesus needed close friends of both genders after all, friends with arms and legs, veins and arteries. But I totally get how God fills those gaps in our lives through his servants or angels on earth, or however you want to describe those special people that just make life worth living. Ed is one such person and so is Celine. There are many more and you know who you are. Perhaps the biggest lesson I learnt from 'Pennygate' was to never underestimate the value of long-standing friendships (and I include my marriage in that) over fleeting attractions. These long-standing friendships, like fine wines, only increase in value with age, becoming a thing of beauty in and of themselves.

Re-entering 'civilian' life felt very strange at first. I had spent my entire adult life in and around Christians and 'churchy' people. In many ways, it was a blessed relief to vacate the bubble and return to the real world of my youth. I suddenly had vast swathes of time available that had previously been taken up by the endless meetings that are a universal feature of church life. I reconnected with my pre-church teenage self, repurchasing all the rock CDs I had sold in a fit of fundamentalist self-righteousness in my early twenties and discovering the delights of digital downloads.

Ed and I still had a sense of guilt about pulling the kids out of church, though, by now, the elder two were more than willing accomplices in our escape from the Church of England. So for a while we tried to do church at home with a simple service I devised with the help of the Sacred Space prayer book. But Carter no longer believed in it all – I don't think everything that happened at St Bart's helped – and the younger two just mucked around. It was stressful and forced and we abandoned it after a few months.

I didn't really want to return to church in any shape or form – I didn't need it to feel close to Jesus – but Ed was missing the spiritual input. I did lots of online research, even emailing a few local churches, explaining that we wanted a family church that was affirming of LGBT people. We didn't receive any replies, as such requirements don't generally fulfil the heteronormative modus operandi of the family church. Then I stumbled upon a church online that met reasonably locally to us in a school. It purported on its website to be welcoming of all, 'whether you're gay or straight'. It looked like the sort of place Ed would like, with modern worship and a foot in the present, if the whizzy website was anything to go by.

So we went to the church in the school one Sunday morning. The pastor, Stephen, was clever and friendly, and one couple in particular – Nick and Sarah – were particularly hospitable. We discovered that they ran the kids' groups and we felt happy leaving the younger two with them for the relevant portion of the service. Kristen was too old to be in Sunday School by that stage, but there was nothing suitable for her age-group, so she helped out with the younger ones. Carter came along once to the service, but hated every second of it and never came again.

The congregation contained some individuals that led me to believe that it was indeed LGBT friendly, without saying more than that. We went for a couple of months but it all came to a head on the Church Weekend at a local holiday park. I could just about sit through the musical worship – it wasn't the music that was off-putting, it was pretty good to be fair – it was just the sight of all those clean-scrubbed couples waving their arms in the air. I just automatically assume happy-clappy Christians hold non-LGBT-affirming views and so it brought back lots of angry memories, which wasn't overly conducive to worshipping. It wasn't that anything particularly out of the ordinary happened, I just felt irked by the simplistic and frankly rather judgemental statements people were expressing in a time of open discussion of Scripture. I felt duty bound to challenge these views, which made me come across as angry and ungracious, and as a result, we got asked by Stephen to have coffee with him that afternoon. The whole saga then spilled out. He was exceedingly compassionate and understanding, but we were clearly on a different translation of the Bible.

I so wanted to find the right church, that I suppose I turned a blind eye to certain giveaway signs of latent fundamentalism! The use of the NIV translation of the Bible (mainly as an iPad app – this was one on trend church), and the choice of worship songs really did give it away. My new friend, Sarah, confirmed my views when we met for coffee one day. It seemed I had misread the ethos of the church from the website, which seemed to lay out the red carpet for the rainbow alliance. And it also transpired that I wasn't the first person to make that assumption. I discussed with Sarah the dangers of misleading people and the hurt and anger it caused an already bruised person, to come along to something they thought was going to be LGBT affirming, only to find the same old 'love the sinner, hate the sin' rhetoric. Such rhetoric is, of course, offensive nonsense. Would you feel loved if you went to dinner at someone's house and they told you they didn't approve of your lifestyle, whilst pouring you a glass of vino? Being LGBT is ontological, it's who you are at your core, it's not an acquired behaviour or a leisure pursuit.

I know that I mightily challenged Stephen the pastor. He went off and read some books I recommended, including the new Steve Chalke download, *A Matter of Integrity*. Unfortunately, he also went off and read some pretty old stuff from the reparative therapy genre, which probably rang truer to his conservative ears and counteracted much of the good stuff outlined by Steve Chalke, Jack Rogers and others (though I'd love to hear otherwise!). However, I was grateful to Stephen for taking the time to challenge his own preconceptions – it was not a trait I had seen much of in either FOB or the C of E.

Stephen was very good to us in that spring/summer 2013 period. Whether his views ultimately changed or not, I don't know, as we're no longer in touch, but he was always willing to listen and did not judge me. And I was a bit of a mess, it has to be said. I had frequent panic attacks over the kids' welfare and social media after all that had happened in the C of E. I also had many sleepless nights, feeling as if I would never be safe again, that I would be dogged by shame for the rest of my life. It was a measure of how damaged and traumatised by the whole episode I was, that over a year later I still thought I would have to watch over my shoulder for the rest of my life, and that I might never get a proper job again. It hardly seems credible two years on, as I juggle a well-paid job with my doctorate studies, that I should have felt so hopeless and so consumed by fear. However, just the faintest reminder of that dark place can transport me back to the hole in the sidewalk[2] in an instant. But if that makes me more vigilant against potholes, then that's maybe not such a bad thing after all.

We did try to support Nick and Sarah in a family home group held at their house, but in the end it was just like stepping back in time to the late 1980s/early 1990s. The same fundamentalist views, espoused by the same fundamentalist types, just cropped up time and time again, and in the end it was a step backwards rather than a step forwards. That said, we met some decent people at the church in the school, of which Nick and Sarah were amongst the best. We also really appreciated Stephen. He had shown integrity and he was a nice guy. We liked him a great deal, but the church wasn't for us.

After that slightly disastrous 'worship on the rebound', we decided to put church on the back burner for the time being. To be honest, it was getting more and more difficult to attend, as DJ had started playing football for a local team, and Ed often refereed their matches. In addition, the older two had various uniformed clubs which often convened on a Sunday. I didn't personally feel the loss at all, as I was beginning to get involved with LGBT faith organisations in London, so I still felt that my spiritual needs were being met.

[2] See *Autobiography in Five Short Chapters* by Portia Nelson, freely available online.

Another Street

Times were a-changin', and no more so than in the first six months of 2013. In January alone, iconic American actress Jodie Foster came out as gay at the Golden Globes and Barack Obama made a historic speech advocating LGBT rights at his inauguration. This side of the pond, Steve Chalke caused shockwaves throughout the evangelical faith community by performing a u-turn on same-sex relationships, publishing *A Matter of Integrity* online. He was closely followed two months later by his telegenic US equivalent, mega-church pastor Rob Bell, one of America's one hundred most influential people. Then in June, Exodus International, the notorious Christian reparative therapy ministry, apologised to the LGBT community and closed its doors in its current format, acknowledging a well-nigh zero gay–straight conversion rate. August 2014 saw much-feted Christian worship leader, Vicky Beeching, come out in the British press, mirroring the decision taken by her Nashville counterpart, Jennifer Knapp, several years previously.

These represented seismic changes in both popular culture and Christian circles, and whenever I attended LGBT Christian events in London, I truly had the sense that I was partaking in history. I had already joined LGCM,[3] the long-standing Christian LGBT activist group, as their CEO at that time, the Revd Sharon Ferguson, had been a real tower of strength in those dark days following Penny's allegations.

Slowly my life began to gather pace again. After a few disastrous early forays back into the world of work (a South American money launderer followed by working in an estate agency – not sure which was the more corrupt!), I secured a temporary job as an administrator for a large local social enterprise, a post which was then made permanent in 2014. I had also used my time away

[3] The Lesbian and Gay Christian Movement, formerly known as the Gay Christian Movement.

from Reader training to familiarise myself with the latest developments in LGBT theology with a view to writing some material for publication. However, I got chatting to an eminent professor of theology and was offered an MPhil/PhD place in February 2014. So within two years of 'D-day', I had secured myself a well-paid job and a doctorate place. God truly does work for the good of those he loves, however badly we love him back. This was a bespoke new life, even down to the picturesque walk to work, a stroll along the riverbank that lifted my spirits after the urban gloom of the estate agency and the many dark nights of the soul.

Whilst I retained membership of LGCM, I pretty much let the other LGBT events/groups in London drop by the wayside. I realised after a while that I really didn't have anything much in common with the people at these events. They were mostly populated by young(ish) gay couples with no kids and a high disposable income. While you heard the odd mention of bisexuality, I found lesbian and gay issues prevailed, especially with the push for marriage equality. It was lonely and tiring going all the way to London on a Saturday to attend an event for a couple of hours, and no one to share it with. I felt guilty leaving Ed with the kids, even though he was supportive of my toe-dipping exercises, and to be honest, I missed them all too much. Ed had no need to worry about these forays to the capital at all – a day spent with LGBT Christians made me long for my 'straight' home life, sat in front of Saturday night telly with the kids and a takeaway curry!

I had also made a few lesbian friends from various churches in my time away from St Bart's. But I didn't really have an awful lot in common with them in terms of lifestyle and outlook on life and those friendships all petered out. My life was just very heteronormative compared to theirs, I suppose.

I have come to realise that I have far more in common with the 'soccer moms' on a Sunday morning than I do with LGBT groups, Christian groups, or indeed LGBT Christian groups. I'm not sure if it's about 'straightness'; I sense it's more about family life. I guess as more and more gay couples adopt, then these gatherings will become more representative of society, in terms of age groups attending and income levels. I also have no interest in mimicking church – I've been there, done that, bought the t-shirt, drank the communion wine.

The older I get, the more I appreciate life's pragmatists over life's idealists – those who accept the practical realities of life and make the best of existing situations. Politically I'm slightly left of centre, but I'm no idealist. Within both the political and theological realm, what offers optimum life and optimum hope is usually the pathway for me. I have felt a strong sense of calling ever since the events of 2012 to share an inclusive gospel with everyday people, wherever it takes me. I have a particular heart for giving voice to the silent 'B' in LGBT, and I harbour a general desire to see justice for all LGBT people, inside or outside of the Church, from all corners of the globe.

Negotiating the terrain between family life and my burgeoning sense of vocation has not been without its own challenges. Both Ed and I are still incredibly twitchy about the events at St Bart's and that, to a large extent, influences how 'vocal' I am about bisexual issues. I not only invite attention on myself by speaking up for bi faith issues; I also implicate Ed and the children in whatever I choose to say or write. That's a significant burden not carried by the majority of gay and lesbian Christians. There's also a lot of very damaged folks within the LGBT faith community. Hurt people hurt – I've learned the hard way that not all LGBT Christians are as discreet or as understanding as one might anticipate from one's fellow travellers on the potholed path.

10

Ninety-Nine Per Cent Perspiration

A study that appeared in the *Journal of Public Health*[1] in January 2015 highlighted that bisexual women have the worst mental health of all sexual minorities. Bisexual women are more likely to suffer poor mental health and psychological distress than lesbians. We are 64 per cent more likely to have eating disorders and 37 per cent more likely to have self-harmed than gay women. We are also 26 per cent more likely to suffer from depression and 20 per cent more likely to have suffered from anxiety. I don't have statistics for the mental health of bisexual Christian women, but I cannot imagine they make for positive reading, given we are less likely to be 'out' than our non-believing sisters and less likely, on the whole, to seek advice or medication for low spirits due to the stigma attached to perceived 'faithlessness' in the Church.

Another study, this time from Canada in 2010,[2] showed that nearly half of bisexual women and over

[1] See http://jpubhealth.oxfordjournals.org/content/early/2015/01/07/pubmed.fdu105.full.
[2] See http://sf-hrc.org/sites/sf-hrc.org/files/migrated/FileCenter/Documents/HRC_Publications/ Articles/Bisexual_Invisibility_Impacts_and_Recommendations_March_2011.pdf.

a third of bisexual men have seriously considered or attempted suicide, compared to just 9.6 per cent of heterosexual women and 7.4 per cent of heterosexual men. The figures for lesbian women stand at 29.5 per cent and gay men, 25.2 per cent. It was noted that bisexual men, are 6.3 times more likely to report lifetime suicidality than heterosexual men and bisexual women 5.9 times more likely than heterosexual women. Again, figures for bisexual people of faith are not available.

I have never attempted suicide, though I confess to once having looked up how many paracetamol it took to successfully overdose, in the aftershock of what happened at St Bart's. I communicated the fact to Hillary Norris, who immediately rang Ed and frightened the living daylights out of him. I have also behaved recklessly, driving my car too fast up the motorway late at night in fits of anger and frustration, and I have self-harmed, though not with cutting – head-butting the wall was my particular forte, born of frustration with my own stupidity. That really freaked one Christian friend out at the height of my head-banging activity. We are no longer in touch. What can I say? So many people, especially Christians, just cannot handle depression and mental illness … until it happens to them or someone close to them. Pretty similar to homosexuality, really. It's all too easy to fire bullets at tin cans until you're part of the display yourself.

So friends have drifted in and out of my life, largely dependent on my mental state at the time. Depression and anxiety, however, are a constant. I'm kind of resigned to the fact that I am likely to be on medication for pretty much the rest of my life.[3] Most of the time, I'm just fine. I'm an extrovert, self-confident, quick-witted kind of person – and so many people would have no idea just how subterranean I can get. By the grace of God, I have never

[3] As I edit this book, I've been 'clean' of SSRIs for a month. I'll keep you posted!

reached the point of no return, though I suspect that has something to do with having three beautiful children and a fantastic husband to consider (and no, I never seriously considered overdosing on paracetamol).

But just getting by as bi can be tough. One PhD student whose thesis I recently picked up opened her research with the statement: 'Bisexuality is a mind-f**k.' It's not the erudite opening sentence I have planned for my eventual doctoral thesis – 'Doing a PhD is a mind f**k' would be my opening gambit of choice! – but I more than get the sentiment.

It *is* very confusing, and I don't know many bi people who would disagree. One minute you have the hots for Scarlett Johansson, the next you're salivating over David Beckham in his Calvin Kleins. Bisexual people are largely invisible, both in the Church and in society as a whole. It's not easy to be 'out', and therefore mentally healthy, when you have a school run to do, or church to attend. Many bisexual people are wives and mothers, with other people to factor in. It's not as simple as just 'being yourself' when being yourself would have a negative effect on those closest to you. I made this point recently at a Stonewall conference, and whilst most of the (younger) people in the room looked at me blankly, two older bisexual men came up to me afterwards and thanked me for my courage in pointing this out.

The vast majority of people are ignorant of bisexuality and have a tendency to over-sexualise the identity, immediately making crass remarks about the frequency and diversity of sexual encounters you are clearly having as a bi person. Inside or outside of a church setting, these are value judgements on you and have an impact not just on your mental health, but on the wellbeing of your dependents. It really is just easier for everyone if you keep your mouth shut about it ... until you die from suffocation.

But as bi campaigner Robyn Ochs recently stated,

being bisexual is quite simply about having a romantic or sexual attraction to more than one gender,[4] it is not about sexual acts, any more than we would insist that a heterosexual person must be sexually active to be classified as straight. Innuendo about adultery and polyamory is never far off when you disclose that you are bisexual.

It's the sheer lack of acknowledgement of bisexuality that's probably the toughest thing to handle, particularly in a faith context. Whilst homosexuality is (almost) becoming acceptable in the mainstream Churches in the UK, so long as you mimic heterosexual marriage and fulfil all the requirements of a middle-class member of the establishment, anything outside of the monosexual[5] norm is simply not up for discussion.

But what are you supposed to do when you need intimacy, romantic and/or sexual, with both sexes, to feel well or 'whole'? The intensity of feeling a bisexual person experiences is not halved or diluted by virtue of being directed at two sexes. The depth of the longing for each gender is the same. As American rock band Living Color note in their track 'Bi', the tension and passion is doubled for dual attracted people.

I'm at a place in my life now where my husband 'gets' what I need to feel well. I have a close female friend with whom I am cuddly, and he is not threatened by that. It takes away nothing from how I feel about him; if

[4] See http://robynochs.com/bisexual/ : 'I call myself bisexual because I acknowledge that I have in myself the potential to be attracted – romantically and/or sexually – to people of more than one sex and/or gender, not necessarily at the same time, not necessarily in the same way, and not necessarily to the same degree.'
[5] Monosexual relates to only being attracted to one gender; it should not be confused with monogamist, which refers to being sexually active with just one person.

anything, it enhances our marriage, as I feel 'weller', as well as being eternally grateful to him for his love and understanding. I have never lied to Ed about my sexuality; he knew all along I was bisexual, but knowing and truly understanding what that means in a relationship context are two different things. It took until our mid-forties, with many disasters along the way, to get to that place. But more about my 'remarkable man' in Chapter 11!

You might be wondering about the title of this chapter. Yes, it alludes to the Thomas Edison quote, that genius comprises of 1 per cent inspiration and 99 per cent … rancid sweat, if I'm quite honest! The problem with taking antidepressants is that as well as having the (obvious) positive effect of shoring up your emotions, they *do* have side-effects. Like thumping great headaches if, perish the thought, you go away without a stash in your toiletry bag. Like giving you a raging thirst, or achy legs. And like sweating for Great Britain! Of course, not everyone will have all these symptoms all the time, but most of us on SSRIs will experience at least one of these.

Mine, as you will have guessed by now, is the night sweats. I never experienced these with fluoxetine (Prozac), but both citalopram (Celexa) and sertraline (Zoloft) have that effect on me. I had a brief fling with citalopram when it became obvious that fluoxetine wasn't even touching the sides during my second big downer in 2012, but it just gave me the sweats without lifting my spirits. Sertraline, which I'm still on now, and likely to remain on long-term at my current 100mg dosage,[6] definitely keeps me on an even keel, though that may be more to do with the high dosage than the chemical composition of the drug. However, I am still suffering from excess perspiration at night-time, which is worse during menstruation or when my body temperature is otherwise elevated.

---

[6] See previous footnote.

Ninety-Nine Per Cent Perspiration

It is quite gross, to be honest, as Ed will absolutely agree. The duvet and sheet stick to my body so that every time I roll over, the bedclothes come with me, leaving me open to accusations of duvet theft. On the rare occasions when Ed summons up the requisite courage to cuddle me, he, too, is in danger of sticking to my flesh and being rolled over with me, like some kind of conjugal pig in a blanket. It is the greatest deterrent ever to polyamory. I think I would simply be too embarrassed to share a bed with anyone other than Ed!

Weirdly, though, and this is where I will gross you out even further, I *like* the smell of Sertra-sweat. It's a different kind of body odour to the usual *eau d'armpit*. There is a sort of comforting musky smell to it, the smell of toil and pain but also victory – a daily reminder that life is hard, but I'm winning the fight. So every morning (I told you this was gross) I like to sniff the damp sheet where I've lain all night, and inhale the smell of sweat and tears. It's almost become a ritual, like I have to brush my lips with seawater every time I go to the beach.

On a more serious note, it's the mental health aspect of being bisexual, every bit as much as the dual attraction side of it, that makes life so complex. It's wonderful in some ways, being bi. It does, on the whole, make life more interesting, emotionally richer, if you like. The kind of ambiguity and psychological suffering that accompanies it does make you more accepting of grey areas and perhaps more sensitive to the suffering of others, especially those traditionally rejected by society. I think I have better relationships with both men and women, too, for being bi. I do not see other women as love rivals, therefore I have a tendency to be supportive rather than bitchy towards my own gender. And I am not falling at the feet of men, as they're not my sole *raison d'être*, as they are for many women – which is good for deflating their egos – which means I can relate to them as friends with ease.

If I had to give advice to church leaders about being bi

– not that they're asking – I'd explain it as follows. Imagine you're living in a country with a one-child policy. You give birth to twins, a boy and a girl. What would feel right and just to you? What would keep you happy and sane? To keep both of them, or to give one up in accordance with the law? Given the choice, I am sure you would elect to keep both of them, and even if you weren't permitted, I'm sure you'd fight tooth and nail and take whatever risks you could to keep them both. If you've had more than one child, you will know already that whilst you may love them differently, your love for each child remains as vast as the ocean. You cannot differentiate between the two; you cannot say, if I had the choice, I'd keep Baby X and give up Baby Y. Both are infinitely precious to you and an irrevocable part of you. And just because they are twins, does that reduce your love for them, to the extent that your combined love for each twin only equates to another person's whole love for their single child? That is a ludicrous suggestion.

Love cannot be quantified or regulated – and that includes love for ourselves, as well as others. Love others *as you love yourself.* I would not expect another person to give up a major part of themselves like sexuality, something they were born with and had no choice over (unless they were called to the monastic life, which is quite a different thing); yet we routinely expect this of bisexual people within the Church. The – frankly – derisory document *Issues in Human Sexuality*, published by the Church of England in 1991, recommends that bisexual people do precisely that. Follow your straight side and all will be well. Take up your cross and deny yourself for Christ. Die to self. Well, I don't see the other 98 per cent of Christians denying their sexuality in this way, committing themselves to a life of (partial) loneliness and frustration, and, frankly, the ones who do are usually sad, dry husks of people, those washed-out joyless old-before-their-time individuals you encounter at many a Christian gathering who have tragically never realised that God is *for* them, not against them. I do not personally know any people who live life to the full (John 10:10) with one hand tied behind their back and a bag over their head, but that's how it feels when you shut down your sexual instincts and your emotions out of some misguided notion of personal holiness. I know, I've been there. As one friend commented, where has Jaime gone?

One accusation constantly thrown at you by other Christians is the adultery question. Doesn't being bisexual involve adultery? Isn't having a relationship with a man and a woman concurrently no different to me cheating on my husband/wife with another man/woman? I would challenge that statement in three ways.

First, being bisexual, as already mentioned, is about being *attracted* to both men and women romantically and/or sexually. It doesn't necessarily mean that you are having dual sexual relations. I would not throw adultery into the ring if someone told me they were heterosexual, so why is this assumption made about bisexual people?

Following on from that, bisexuality is an identity, like heterosexuality. It is the expression of *who we are* not *what we do*. You needn't be having sexual relations with anyone to identify as heterosexual; the majority of non-sexually active heterosexuals still maintain their right to be identified as straight and to operate within heteronormative parameters (for example, talking about who you fancy off the telly, commenting on the hot new person at work, etc.).

Thirdly, what is missing in the bisexual Christian's life is the ability to hold a bisexual identity – and a clear sense of personal identity is imperative to mental health. Bisexuality is largely invisible in church publications and doctrinal debate, which means acknowledgement of bisexual people and support for bisexual issues are missing in our churches and faith communities. It is as if we don't really exist, that we are just a figment of our own imagination. Heterosexual people (and increasingly gay people) can express their identity through the lives they are openly able to lead. The monosexual[7] person is able to express their monosexual identity through everyday life with their existing partner. But a bisexual person cannot express their dual sexual identity through living entirely as a hetero- (or homo-) sexual person. And that leads to repression and ultimately health issues.

Identity is not about sex; it is about how we perceive ourselves, how others perceive us and our place in the world. There are clubs and organisations, civil rights and – increasingly – marriage liturgies for both hetero- and homosexual people. But there is no public acknowledgement in any tangible sense of a bisexual identity, much beyond dating sites and sex advisory clinics. Believe me, there are enough of us around to prove this is *not* just a bunch of over-sexed sinners in denial.

Denying your sexuality and with it your sexual identity doesn't work. Believe me, I've tried. No one could have tried harder than me to be straight and monosexual. It just made me ill, as friends warned me it would. I am happier, healthier and more self-confident since I accepted my sexuality and stopped trying to pretend I was anything other than a lover of men and women. That doesn't mean I need to be out having sex with both men and women; it does mean, however, that I acknowledge my need to give and receive love from women, as well as from my husband, in order to feel whole. I might be physically closer to another woman than a heterosexual woman might be. My hugs might just last that second or two longer. But the nature of the love exchanged is a matter between God and myself, in consultation with Ed and with any potential partner; it has nothing to do with

[7] Just to reiterate, a monosexual person is someone who is only sexually attracted to one gender.

anybody else, just as other people's spiritual welfare or health management strategies are nothing to do with me. I do not make assumptions about other people's sex lives, so why should they make assumptions about mine?

What causes bisexuality? Is it genetic or acquired? If I knew the answer to that, I'd be writing a very different kind of book today, with greatly increased royalties! Recent reports in the news suggest that the majority of straight women are bisexual, with the ability to be aroused by both sexes.[8] There is also some evidence that over-exposure to testosterone in the womb for a baby girl may result in more masculine attributes, including sexual attraction towards women.[9] I believe my mother might have been hospitalised for pre-eclampsia when she was pregnant with me, which may have involved testosterone-based drugs. But that seems tenuous to me. Other than needing to be held by women, and enjoying a game of football more than most, there's nothing to separate me from your average straight woman (though that concept itself is negligible as we learn more and more about the fluidity of human sexuality). I do look back at some of my childhood photos around the age of four or five, where my mother appeared to have taken me to the barbers instead of the local salon for a short back and sides, and wonder if she had sufficiently affirmed my girlhood! But then that's going down the parental blame route, and I'm not sure that's either rational or fair. It also suggests bi-/homosexuality is an aberration and I'm uncomfortable with that idea.

On the whole, I don't think I really subscribe to the nurture argument, though I am sympathetic to the idea that nobody is totally straight and it is simply society that has named and categorised sexualities. While certain events along the journey of life may have nudged me in a more bisexual direction, such as attending an all-girls' school at

[8]   See http://www.bbc.co.uk/news/health-34744903
[9]   See footnote 8..

the crucial development stage of eleven to sixteen, or the lack of close bonding with my mother – even the absence of a sister – logic tells me that there must be thousands upon thousands of women who attended single-sex schools who have not 'turned out' bisexual. And there will undoubtedly be many more who are not particularly close to their mums or who don't have a sister to confide in, who end up monosexual.

I think it's probably genetic, part of God's diverse plan. Either that, or we're all bisexual really, as the cliché goes, just to varying degrees. If I could change my sexuality, or if God wanted to change it for me, I think it would have happened by now. God knows, I've tried hard enough. And although I shouldn't use my sexuality to justify irresponsible behaviour, I *can* use my sexuality to bring understanding to a world that uses binary thinking (black/white; gay/straight; Muslim/Christian) to justify and maintain positions of power in society. Life is not black and white; people are not black and white; human sexuality is not black and white. Negotiation, compromise and hearing the other side are crucial to the success of a civilised society, as is adult behaviour. If human beings celebrated and focused on what unites us, rather than what divides us and makes us different, the world would be a far kinder and better place to be. But we use difference – ethnic, sexual, socio-economic – to create power bases for ourselves and to maintain privileged positions. That is why proportional representation is still not a reality in British politics. Proportional representation would require the party in power to concede an element of control – and people in positions of power are rarely up for that. The Church is no different. Why would straight white men (or straight black men in Africa) want to allow diversity in the ranks if it threatened their privileged positions in the echelons of power?

From that perspective, I can fully understand why bisexuality is such a nightmare for the Church of England, or indeed any Church, with the exception of the Quakers and the Metropolitan Community Church, who seem to have the structures to contain diversity. Homosexuality is not necessarily welcome in the mainstream denominations, but at least it isn't messy like bisexuality or transgender. Gay people, so long as they are in a monogamous, committed relationship, can largely find acceptance in the faith community – though the battle is far from over. And if they can't, then there is a clearly defined lesbian and gay alternative faith community to meet their needs. Bisexual or gender-fluid people, however, defy category. And categories are needed to organise people. And people need organising to maintain control. But love cannot be controlled. It is an abundance of feeling that resists any attempt to contain it. Or indeed heal it.

It is the lack of a 'natural habitat' for bisexual Christians that is a massive source of tension and has undoubtedly contributed to my own mental health issues. The LGBT faith community may include my sexuality in its name or in its straplines, but I have met more bisexual people through 'secular'[10] organisations or within academia than through any LGBT faith group. That is a source of sadness to me, but hopefully God will use me to redress the balance, when the time is right to speak out. I have also met several bisexual Christian women who are either in denial about the fact, or who refuse to publicly acknowledge their bisexuality. That doesn't help, either, though I fully understand why they might not want to, given the levels of ignorance and prejudice about dual attraction.

---

[10] You will note that I have a malaise with terms such as 'non-Christian and secular'. It is my personal belief that all people are made in God's image. Some people are conscious of this or choose to recognise this; others do not. I do not personally believe we have either the inside knowledge or the right to categorise other people according to our own preconceptions of where they stand with God.

However, I believe the tide is beginning to turn. Stonewall's acknowledgement in 2014 that they have not been as supportive as they might have been of bisexual people will be influential in how bisexuality is perceived by both politicians and other LGBT organisations. Ruth Hunt, current CEO of Stonewall, is fantastically good news for the 'secular' and 'Christian' LGBT community alike. As an 'out' Catholic, she has the ability lacked by her predecessors to unite two historically divergent communities into one effective political movement against inequality.

However, it is not only my mental health that is affected by my sexuality; it obviously impacts on my husband and, to a lesser degree, my children. Ed, as you will have gathered by now, is an incredibly sagacious, supportive and loving individual. Of course he has been badly hurt by my various indiscretions and the ensuing fallout, and I carry a great deal of guilt about that. In addition, I feel a certain burden of guilt towards my eldest child, who also suffers from depression. There is some medical evidence that children of depressed parents are more prone to mental health issues themselves,[11] which is perhaps not surprising, but still doesn't ease the responsibility you feel on their behalf, as a parent suffering from depression. No person is an island; we need to help others feel whole for the benefit of everyone. That's what good citizenship is about.

[11] See http://www.huffingtonpost.com/peggy-drexler/when-moms-depressed-what_b_8559030. html

11

Portrait of a Marriage
1996–

Ed and I will have been married twenty years this September, which is quite an achievement these days. I believe we have a fantastic marriage with open lines of communication and love and laughter in equal measure. It has not been easy, but we knew it wouldn't be. We got married on the understanding that it would be complex owing to my sexuality, and true to form, it has been pretty rocky at certain points – though perhaps more on account of my mental health than my sexuality (though of course my sexuality and mental health are inextricably linked). It's not all been about my shortcomings, though. Ed is the first to admit he can be cantankerous, unduly anxious about money, and rather demanding in certain aspects. And of course, kids add their own unique contribution to the mix, especially as they hit the teenage years.

For the vast majority of the time, however, it is much like any other healthy marriage. We sometimes disagree, but are able to come to a decision without needing to activate the 'male headship' clause. We have learnt, through trial and error, how to compromise both in our marriage and in parenting to achieve optimal equilibrium at home. We have brought up three self-confident, mature children, who, whilst not without fault or issues, make us proud and grateful to God on a daily basis. They are allowed to be themselves, as is abundantly clear, and for me that is one of the most precious gifts you can give a child. It puts them at ease with themselves, because they know who they are, enabling them to find their place in the world and function well in adulthood. I only wish my parents had given me that gift; it could have saved decades of unnecessary suffering. But how many parents in the 1970s and 1980s would have supported an LGBT child?

Certainly, I am blessed to have met Ed. We have so much in common. I am Scottish by birth, he is a Scotophile, with a love for the novels of A. L. Kennedy, the music of Capercaillie and, of course, me! We both like topical news shows, Scandi crime and military history. We both love travel and visiting new places, but also curling up in front of the football with a bottle of Becks and a Domino's pizza. We were friends long before we were married, and so there are never uncomfortable gaps in the conversation – shutting Ed up is more of a challenge!

Differences? Ed takes his coffee Whoopi Goldberg, I'm a Julie Andrews. He likes doors open, I like them shut. He likes the radio on; I crave the sound of silence. He likes bright lights; I prefer a cosy ambience. He likes shopping; I prefer sleeping. But these are small things, the normal stuff of married life.

We are living proof that mixed-orientation marriages needn't end in disaster. Where there is genuine love and understanding – for better, for worse, in sickness and in mental health – there is a way forward. Where there is respect for difference and a mutual desire for wholeness, there is the promise of many years to come. And where there is faith in a loving God who created us all uniquely in his image, there is hope.

Will we go back to church? The jury's still out on that one. I, for one, do not miss the massive drain on our time it represented, with the interminable meetings and inward-looking events that largely do little to change injustices in our society.

Ed is not so cynical about church, though there is no way he will ever countenance returning to the Church of England. I think we are both open to attending some kind of faith community in the future, so long as it is theologically inclusive, sufficiently intellectual, and grounded in reality. It will probably be easier when the kids have all left home and we have more freedom. I'm in no rush. Having sacrificed a quarter of a century to church life, I am sure God understands my need to take some time out to process, reflect and recover from all that happened, to let my scars heal. It's taken nearly ten years for my stretch marks to disappear, after all! Forgiving myself for the events of 2012 has proved far more difficult than extending forgiveness to others.

Our faith remains real, even if we don't engage in spiritual discussion or prayer together very often. I have never felt the need for contrivances like 'quiet times' – God is in me and around me at all times, the channels of communication are always open. I can't speak for Ed on that score; but everything about the way he comports himself at home and in public tells me that he is increasing in grace and wisdom as he grows older, surely more of an indication of spiritual fecundity than church attendance.

I am always incredulous at these middle-aged Christian couples you meet who remain steeped in the same simplistic evangelical faith package they first bought into thirty years ago. It's the Christian equivalent of rereading your Noddy books into adulthood, because they're comforting and familiar, with goodness and evil simply defined for you. Never underestimate the pulling power of certainty and closure! But, as I said earlier, that's what happens when you become so immersed in church culture. It almost lobotomises you. It is entirely possible to spend your entire life in this homogenous pseudo-world, where every evening is taken up by meetings and church events – tail-chasing exercises – and to remain barely touched by the world revolving and evolving outside.

I will never say I am glad about what happened at St Bart's – the shame I felt over my actions was crippling, the pain surrounding the allegations and that evil anonymous letter was visceral. But I *am* glad to have escaped the strange parallel universe that was church life. I am happier and healthier and more fit for purpose now that I am fully engaged with the complexities and compromises of real life.

Where's that bit in the Bible about progressing from milk to solids?[1] Neither Ed nor I really understand how people cannot evolve spiritually and take a more circumspect view of life as they grow older. There are no evil goblins in the woods converting our children into homosexuals, but there are plenty of goblins in the worldwide Church misusing the Bible to queer-bash LGBT people.

I love the Bible, but I no longer make an idol of it. Reading Scripture is one way of meeting God. But a large part of meeting with God is done through communication with him and through life itself. Otherwise we're just people who endlessly pass our Driving Theory Test without taking the practical exam. Getting 'out there' on the road is where you actually learn to drive, to gain awareness of others, to find your position on the road alongside other drivers, and to adapt to a range of different circumstances (and get disciplined for taking liberties!). The map or satnav doesn't always take you to the right place; sometimes a new road has been built since. Sometimes you ask the wrong person and they misdirect you. I could go on with the driving analogies. My point is, we worship a living God. He has the power to change things. It is my personal belief that the seismic changes in Western society regarding LGBT rights are a move of the Spirit. For me it is no coincidence that so many leading lights in politics, popular culture and

[1] Hebrews 5:12–14.

evangelical Christianity have spoken out in favour of equality for LGBT people in the past few years. God is good, God is just, so goodness and justice *will* prevail.

How do I see our personal future panning out? I feel that having survived the pain and scandal that erupted at St Bart's, Ed and I can pretty much handle most things. We did discuss (or rather, I did) the big 'D' in the immediate aftermath of what happened with Penny. At that juncture, I could see nothing but a long drawn-out future where I hurt Ed over and over again with my romantic indiscretions. But at the end of the day, I just couldn't conceptualise a life without him. The ties are simply too strong, the love too deep. And he feels the same way. It's not as if he walked into this marriage with his eyes shut.

However, I did promise myself one thing during a bleak Easter break in Scotland, following the episode with Penny in 2012. As I stood on a windswept beach on the North Sea coast, feet away from a grieving Ed, I picked up a large red sandstone pebble and clutched it tightly in my palm. I promised myself that I would sort this pain inside, one way or another, wherever that took me – though hopefully not away from Ed. I could not go on like this any more. I still have that stone; it lives inside the pocket of my winter coat, as a fixed reminder to love myself, as well as Ed. I do the latter far better when I pay heed to the former.

I have largely resolved the pain inside through the grace of God and the people he has placed in my life – and things with Ed are better than ever. God fashions our journeys in strange, mysterious and bespoke ways. No two experiences of God working in lives are ever quite the same. We share our stories to offer comfort to our fellow travellers, walking a similar path to ours, but, at the end of the day, it's my personal walk of faith for which I am fully responsible and answerable to God for.

12

Dust Down the Shoes

I have a beautiful Japanese bowl. It is mended where it once broke. I once saw some new pieces of the same ware in a shop, and they were not so beautiful. The glaze seemed too shiny. My first reaction was to denounce the debasement of a fine old craft. On consideration, I realized what was different was not how the bowls were made. My bowl has been used, and that has given it the rich glow that the new bowls lacked. Even being broken has not harmed either its beauty or its usefulness. Japanese traditionally have treasured priceless old tea things that have been broken and repaired with gold; the place where they were broken now gleams proudly, and the utensil is even more valuable.

Richard Cleaver[1]

I am going to share a secret with you now. Today, as I write this concluding chapter in my story, I have been suspended from work for six weeks and six days.

They say what doesn't kill you makes you stronger and I am very much stronger after the incident at St Bart's. Never again will I let someone else's bullying tactics,

[1] From 'A Note on Using Scripture' in *Know My Name: A Gay Liberation Theology* (Westminster John Knox Press, 1995).

Dust Down the Shoes

however senior they are, deny me my right to be heard and respected, whatever I have or have not done. So I fought back when my current line manager told me I was going to be formally disciplined for something I hadn't done, or at least not in the way she claimed I had. I joined the biggest trade union I could find and made full use of the pen (or the keyboard, to be precise) to defend myself against the accusations (so much mightier than the sword in the business world). So I am now at home, on paid 'gardening leave' while they decide what to do with me.

These forty-eight days have afforded me the first extended period of paid holiday ever. I feel kind of guilty for having enjoyed my period of suspension, but in truth, it's been a real blessing, enabling me to get this story down, led I believe by the Spirit, since it has flowed so effortlessly.

I'm not sure whether this is an omen or not, but serendipitously, I sat on my mobile phone whilst I was driving a few weeks ago. Somehow, my bottom clicked the Bible app on my phone and went straight to Mark 6:11, which reads:

> And if any place will not receive you and they will not listen to you, when you leave, shake off the dust that is on your feet as a testimony against them.[2]

Does this mean I'm about to be sacked? I'll keep you posted. Perhaps it refers to a more significant ministry I believe I'm about to embark upon, where, without doubt, I will not be received or listened to by many. Mine is not a message that comes neatly packaged in easily digestible chunks. People are just beginning to get their heads around homosexuality in our Churches, let alone dual attraction. As messages go, it's a complex carbohydrate. One thing is clear to me: these trials have been sent to

---

[2] English Standard Version, not NIV!

build perseverance, to toughen me up. I guess it's basic Newtonian physics, but when we do anything with force, we provoke an opposite reaction. When we go out with love in our hearts, we invite hatred. When we go out with confidence, others attack us out of insecurity. When we try and spread an inclusive Gospel of love, we meet with exclusive gospels of hatred.

However convincing their 'scriptural' arguments, I believe that God is love – it says that in the Bible, too. So I believe that the correct Gospel is the one that offers optimal hope and optimal love to the optimal amount of people. I believe in a generous God and an inclusive message for all people who love, and who long to be loved back. Because to love sacrificially, whole-heartedly and without limit is to reflect God.

So what about the future? It is my personal view that there will be no middle ground in our Churches very soon. Remember that hoary old C. S. Lewis quote that gets trotted out every single Alpha course? The one about Jesus – Son of God or madman? Basically, the argument runs, there can be no 'good moral teacher' rhetoric around Jesus. He was either who he claimed to be, i.e. the Son of God, or he was a lunatic for claiming he was. And lunatics do not generally make good moral teachers, as a quick glance at the God channel will tell you.

Well, similarly, there's no option of a middle ground in church doctrine when it comes to human sexuality. Either you take the gospels literally and see all relationships outside of heterosexual marriage/conjoining as forbidden, or you take a contextual view of Scripture, as being subject to cultural norms at that time and place in history and to the limits of the authors' knowledge. There is no logic, to my mind, in a position that accepts gay relationships so long as they are not consummated. It is the sexual equivalent of inviting a guest to sit at your table but not allowing him or her to eat. Crazy and cruel. If they're not welcome at the table, then in Jesus' name, don't issue them with an invite. It's just plain mean. It's either no to gay relationships *period* or yes to consummated gay relationships. Spare me the irrational middle-ground fudge that pleases nobody and hurts so many.

For me, it's desperately disappointing that while many clergy keep up to date with developments in theology concerning the role of women, for example, few keep up with theological advances in our understanding of human sexuality. There is so much high-quality, academically rigorous, well-thought-out material out there to argue the case for an affirming reading of Scripture for LGBT Christians, yet our church hierarchies refuse to engage at any meaningful level with such research, preferring to maintain their privileged position within the status quo – to the severe detriment of others. This even when it is clear lesbian, gay and bisexual clergy exist under their very noses. I met a couple of closeted Readers and clergy during my time in the C of E; it makes me sad to think of the limitations they have imposed on their own personal health and happiness through adherence to a falsely prescribed gospel of bondage.

Time and time again we hear of militant Christians whose views on homosexuality have changed through the sudden coming out of a close friend or family member. When we are confronted with the reality of someone who cannot, with all the best intentions and prayer ministry in the world, fall in love with the opposite sex, and we witness their loneliness and suffering first hand, we cannot help but question why a loving God would want that person to continue in this vein. What on earth is the purpose for their life, remaining in bondage to an ideal they can never live up to?

I heard a very sad story some time ago from an evangelical Christian acquaintance of mine. I had challenged some fairly fundamentalist views he held on homosexuality. It had opened up a whole can of worms and it later emerged that his father had committed suicide following an arrest for cottaging. He could not forgive his father for putting his family through hell; I pointed out the hell his father must have been going through to have looked for love in such a lonely place to start off with, let alone taking his own life. 'But Scripture says ...', he argued back.

Personally, I do not believe that playing fundamentalists at their own game is a fruitful endeavour (though US LGBT theologian Matthew Vines may beg to differ). We can argue over the meanings of the seven clobber passages until the sacrificial bulls come home, but at the end of the day, whether *arsenokoitai* in 1 Corinthians 6:9 refers to 'top' male partners in gay sex, homosexuals in general or bisexual married men is neither here nor there. Whether the women in Romans 1 are temple prostitutes or not, and whether they are engaging in lesbian sex or heterosexual anal sex, is open to interpretation. But surely at the heart of the Gospel is the figure of Jesus Christ, who proactively sided with the oppressed, the underdogs, the unloved and disenfranchised? And actually, what (and who) is served by debating God's views on anal sex, submissive males or temple prostitutes in first-century Greek culture? As I write this chapter, 129 people have been murdered just across the English Channel from us in Paris by Islamic extremists. I think God may just be a little more concerned about religious hatred than where a few harmless blokes stuck their willies nearly two thousand years ago. And so should we be.

There is nothing in the ethos or general context of the gospels to suggest that Jesus would condemn two same-sex people in love, who were doing nothing to harm anyone else (and indeed, one interpretation of the healing of the centurion's servant in Luke 7 is that the servant is clearly the Roman guard's lover, so beset with grief is the centurion). However, there is a great deal in the gospels to suggest today's Pharisees – right-wing Christian fundamentalists – face the wrath of God for their hard-hearted attitudes towards others whose only sin is to behave in accordance with the laws of humanity.[3]

I firmly believe that we have no right to pronounce judgement on anyone until we have walked a mile in their shoes – and even then the road conditions may have changed. Take abortion, for example. I cannot say hand on heart that I would *not* be straight off to the GP for the morning-after pill if I was raped by a stranger in the street. Some would call that murder of an unborn child; I would call it damage limitation, when I have a husband and three other children to consider. I'm not trying to shock anyone, but the point I am making is this: since I cannot be sure what I would do in that scenario, it is not appropriate for me to judge another woman who elects to have a termination. Similarly, until you know what it's like to ache, really ache, for another woman or another man to hold you, then you really have no right to presume superior insight into their situation, let alone claim to speak for God. Bisexuality is complex, confusing and frequently painful – it's why bisexual people have the worst mental health of all sexual minorities.[4]

Having witnessed three of my close friends from university die of cancer, and having seen my own mental health disintegrate from the lack of compassion of some hard-hearted individuals at church, I no longer have the time nor inclination to let ignorance or negativity drag me down. I once read some invaluable advice in a self-help book: the moment you devote yourself to one person, you immediately make yourself unavailable for at least one other, potentially many more. There are not an ever-expanding number of hours in the day. So choose carefully what you devote your energy to. Negative people and dead-end causes can use up all your energy reserves,

---

[3] 1 Corinthians 10:13: 'No temptation has overtaken you that is not common to man' (ESV).
[4] See statistics on p.156.

leaving you with nothing in the tank for the people who really need you or matter to you. Or at least that's my excuse for sidestepping life's moaners and complainers!

I told you in Chapter 5 about the broken jug. Well, I did have a spectacular fall from grace, and yes, it was very public and I was brought before (ecclesiastical) judge and jury. I certainly felt at the time that my whole being – body and soul – had been shattered into tiny pieces and that I would never be whole again. But it wasn't, not completely, and I've survived. And, as the gay anthem goes, I *will* survive.

There is a beauty in the cracks in our human make-up. As the quote that starts this chapter tells us, the Japanese revere a broken vessel that bears the scars of life, over and above a perfect, newly glazed model. They even highlight the cracks in the glaze with gold. I have always thought it preferable to hide my mistakes and my shortfalls. I felt that I needed to appear clever and in control as part of my witness to others, but also, let's face it, out of sheer vanity. Now I see that it is the embarrassing mistakes that we have made, the pain and the sorrow etched on our faces, that give us character, that make us human and accessible to others. We cannot spread the love of God unless others can relate to us. God is in our broken spirits, in the shame that gouges, in the grooves of the furrowed brow, in the wrinkles of age, but also in the laughter lines around our eyes. Like precious gold.

I will close this book with another serendipitous anecdote: I was filling my car up with fuel at the local Sainsbury's a few days ago, feeling a bit rubbish about the whole work situation, when a silver estate car pulled up at the pump in front of me. The registration was KBO.

Keep buggering on.

I refilled my tank; I *will* survive.

Epilogue

Well, readers, I did get sacked, on 20 November 2015 to be precise. My bottom prophesied correctly.

On the very same morning, I learnt that I had obtained a substantial grant from a large American sexuality think-tank to engage in faith and bisexuality research in the USA. Within half an hour of receiving notification of this, Darton, Longman and Todd emailed me the exciting news that this very manuscript had been accepted for publication. God was speaking loud and clear. Even my rational husband with his Thomasian tendencies could not deny it.

I have even made it back to church this Christmas. Ed wanted to go; it hadn't felt like Christmas for him these past few years without it. The local Bangladeshi restaurant was a poor substitute, if an excellent accompaniment. I agreed, so long as we could attend the church of my good friend, the Revd Eddi Nevin, an old supporter from my Reader training days, whose church was at a safe distance, yet still within a half-hour radius. It was still Church of England, but I trusted the priest implicitly. Eddi had travelled the journey with me from trainee Reader to semi-suicidal wreck and was still there. That meant a lot. And anyone who wears fashion tights and red heels beneath a cassock deserves my full and un-adulterous admiration.

Ed liked her; I knew he would. Maybe we'll go again,

perhaps at Easter, like good occasional Christians. Meanwhile, I continue to enjoy the support of my university chaplain, the Revd Christina Messi, to whom Eddi introduced me. While the C of E continues to put up significant barriers to LGBT people of faith, it cannot be denied that some of the Christian clerics/leaders who have given me most support – Richard Newborne, Geraint Boyce, Olivia Fenton-Hayes, Tracey Byrne of LGCM, Eddi Nevin, Christina Messi – are all Anglican.

As I write this Epilogue, James Corden is being interviewed by Chris Evans on *TFI Friday*. He is speaking about his decision to host *The Late Late Show* in the USA. Corden says to Evans: 'It's better to take a risk and get it wrong, than not take a risk and spend your whole life regretting it.'

The message of the sermon at the Carol Service at Eddi's church was simply this: *do not be afraid*. Trust in God, however outlandish it seems, because amazing things can happen when you ignore the risks, rise above the fear and make that leap of faith. Just watch.

Appendices

Open the Box, 21 January 2012

*This is a short talk I gave to a local women's group.
You can see that I am beginning to feel suffocated by
the evangelical Christian faith in this. The irony of this
being preached shortly before the events of April 2012 at
St Bart's should not go unnoticed either.*

Last October I paid a family visit to South Wales with my
three children. Surprisingly, it was raining, so we took
refuge in the National Waterfront Museum in Swansea. We
wandered upstairs, where there are always lots of hands-
on children's activities, suitable for my six-year-old son. In
the middle of the floor was a haphazard arrangement of
around two dozen small wicker boxes with hinged lids. I
can best describe them as the sort of 1940s pigeon-carrier
boxes you sometimes see in museums and newsreel.
Assuming this was a recent addition to the many touchy-
feely interactive museum items, my son and his grandma
proceeded to stack up the boxes then have great fun
knocking them to the ground. *Some cross-generational
interaction, how lovely,* I gushed inwardly, taking out
my camera. But as I set up the photo, a very stern young
woman appeared on the screen, in a floaty skirt and several
floaty scarves. She had a look of abject horror on her face.
'Please!' she gasped. 'These boxes are part of an
exhibit!'

Unbeknown to us, the top floor of the museum was also being used to show artistic works by students from the local art college. This arrangement of boxes was not a children's play item, but an exhibit of unique artistic merit. I forget its title, possibly 'Basket Cases Through the Ages', or something of that ilk.

My pragmatic Scottish mother looked at the student as if she was from another planet; my six-year-old just looked confused. My daughter ran away, embarrassed, my elder son and I hid behind a display cabinet! The student then pulled open a yellow ring-binder and proceeded to studiously rearrange the wicker boxes according to a clearly detailed design spec. She even took out some kind of measuring device to check the exact angle of the boxes against her plan, to ensure they were haphazardly arranged to perfection.

Now, I am not a cultural philistine, far from it. And I have even been known, on occasion, to wear a floaty skirt. But as I mused upon Basketgate, as it came to be known within the family, something struck me as profoundly significant about this whole episode. And it was this.

Are we not guilty, at times, of creating an art exhibit of our faith, something that we present to others, static and fixed, not to be queried or challenged? And are we not guilty at times, perhaps in the desire to feel settled within, to have theological closure, of viewing the Bible as a closed book, with nothing personal or new to say to us?

Something else struck me about the boxes, too. Sometimes we arrange ourselves at a precise angle, too, don't we? Perhaps it's the worldly desire for identity, the desire to present ourselves in a certain way. I'm a liberal charismatic mother of three and an ex-biker – what are you? But surely to walk truly with God is to be at the whim of his geometry set? Degree by degree he moves us into the place where he wants us ... if we let him. We don't want to be putting ourselves in boxes.

Appendices

This time of year presents us with a wonderful sense of freshness, from the freshness of the wind to the exciting freshness of the new journal or pocket diary, with its clean, inviting pages. It's a season of fresh starts, a land of opportunity, if we let it.

What's in God's gift box for each of us in 2012? Maybe some of us long to know our gifting, the unique talent that God gives all of us, wonderfully and fearfully made in his name. Maybe others of us long to be free to unleash the recognised gift within. Maybe we feel that lid on the cage is well and truly locked on the outside and we need help to be set free. But maybe, just maybe, it opens from within, like that door Jesus invites us to open to him. Maybe we are our own jailers.

One of my favourite verses from Scripture is this, from Jeremiah 15:16: 'When your words came I ate them, they were my joy and my heart's delight'. Or, as *The Message* puts it: 'When your words showed up, I ate them – swallowed them whole. What a feast!' Don't you just love *The Message*?!

There is a very real sensation in Scripture that we are meant to tuck into our faith, to open the lid of the tuck-box and feast on the contents. I believe we are also called to share our tuck, like kids at school, share what we've learnt from one another, mutually grow in our faith and break out of self-imposed identities God never gave us in the first place. Faith that doesn't draw others in, that isn't open to scrutiny, challenge and interaction, is not faith but an artifact, a pretty box.

A perhaps more famous Scripture, Psalm 34, exhorts us to: 'Taste and see that the Lord is good'. We've all probably feasted enough in the carnal sense at Christmas; now is the time for some spiritual feasting as we start the New Year. If Christ says, 'I have come that you may have life, and life to the full', does not that imply a sense of freedom, of expansion, but also of satiation, of realised opportunity? Christ knocks at the door and asks us to open up, not stand and admire the fine craftsmanship of the door furniture. We are to devour God's word, digest his promises, chew the cud, work out our salvation.

'See, I am doing a new thing ... do you not perceive it?' – God's own words to the Israelites via the prophet Isaiah (Isaiah 43:19). We worship a God who longs to do new things in our lives, to make inroads in our spiritual deserts and streams in our spiritual wastelands.

Use today, use the prayer-time, use the silence, use the conversation, to let God in. Open the box. We worship a God who sent his Son down to earth to be with us, among us, around us, inside us, physically, tangibly, not admired from a distance. And you are more than welcome to rearrange my boxes if you want! Amen.

(Note: I had a small display of stacking boxes – this was not some dubious figurative reference!)

Cut Down to Size, 6 April 2012

This was the sermon I preached on Good Friday 2012, in the middle of the painful business with Penny. It is clear just how broken I am feeling, and also how my theology was changing. The talk was based on the story, 'The Three Trees'.

When I was a child, I wanted to be the Bionic Woman, played by the actress Lindsay Wagner. Do you remember her? She was the Six Million Dollar Man's girlfriend and they fought to protect the world against evil. I had a Lindsay Wagner doll. You lifted up flaps of flesh in her leg and her arm to reveal her bionic mechanisms. If you turned her head, her bionic ear made a pinging noise.

Appendices

When I wasn't tearing around the garden in a blue boiler suit being Lindsay Wagner, I was pretending to be Evel Knievel. He was the stunt motorcyclist who jumped over rows of double-decker buses in his star-spangled Harley. Later on in life I had a motorbike, though I never managed to clear any buses on it. I used to park it three doors up, so my parents didn't find out when they visited. They still don't know to this day I owned a Yamaha 500. So I suppose I wanted to be a kind of amalgam of the two, Bionic Woman Stunt Motorcyclist, Lindsay Knievel. Or Evel Wagner. Take your pick.

As an adult, what we aspire to changes – hopefully – though a little bit of me still wants to be Evel Wagner, bionic stunt motorcyclist! I'd like to be seen as someone with integrity and compassion, someone who brings hope to others. A tall tree pointing to God, not a weed in the pathway or a thorn in the side. Maybe you have similar dreams.

Our story today – call it a traditional folktale or a modern-day parable – has many interpretations. Look online and you'll find a plethora of them. To me, the Three Trees speaks of dreams and aspirations – and God's plan for our lives. The first tree aspires to beauty. It longs to be a beautiful treasure chest containing precious jewels. The second tree aspires to physical prowess. It longs to be the strongest ship in the world. The third tree doesn't want to be made into anything. Instead it wishes to be the tallest tree in the world, so that when people look at it, their eyes are drawn upwards to heaven. It longs to remind people of God. A laudable aim, you may think. There are various interpretations of the third tree. Some say it is the tree with the correct aims and doesn't deserve to be chopped down. I don't share that interpretation and I'll tell you why in a minute.

One day, for no apparent reason, three mysterious woodcutters – we could perhaps say a Trinity of woodcutters – come and chop down the three trees. Imagine the vain tree's disgust when it is made not into a beautiful treasure chest but a mundane feeding trough fit only for the farmyard. Similarly, the second tree is not fashioned into a warrior of the seas, but a humble old fishing boat, into which smelly fish would be tossed. The most shameful fate awaits the third tree, which isn't even made into anything, simply chopped into beams and left behind in the yard. All the tall tree wanted to do was point to God. Instead it had been chopped into bits, cut down to size, seemingly left behind.

But the three trees have not been abandoned. Instead God has used them for his glorious purposes. He had a plan for each of them all along, a plan infinitely more important than the dreams they had concocted for themselves. The first tree would become the manger that held the most precious treasure ever, the Christ child. The second tree would become the fishing boat carrying the King of Heaven and Earth, in which he performed one of his greatest miracles. And for the third tree, the most glorious fate of all: it became the cross on which the Prince of Glory died to bring salvation to the world.

There is a clear message in this tale. In many ways, it is the simple message we give the children: we all have plans for our lives, but God's plan for our lives is better, so much better.

But as adults we need perhaps to investigate at a deeper level. And please be very aware that this is only my take on the story, you may go off and see different things in this tale, if indeed it speaks to you at all. For me, this story tells me that any plans we have for our lives which do not involve Jesus at the centre are doomed to be cut down. I don't know if you noticed, but all three trees hold or contain Jesus in some way. The manger holds the baby Jesus, the boat holds the adult Jesus, the cross holds the dying Jesus. We are to hold

Christ at the centre of our lives. Our bodies are to be vessels to be filled with Christ, not ourselves, dwellings for his Holy Spirit. If they're not, we'll be chopped down like the trees and remoulded, or pruned, like the rotten branches in the biblical parable.

This whole service has a very arboreal theme, you will have noticed. And do you know, I even wrote this sermon at Oak Cottage, the home of some very good friends of mine, surrounded by fields of trees. Both our Passion readings today contain tree or woodland imagery. In the Suffering Servant passage, Christ is described as a tender shoot, a root. A crown of thorns is placed on Christ's head. And of course, he is nailed to a cross, one of three crosses, and left on the hillside. Three crosses, made possibly from three trees.

And it is interesting that Jesus is described as a tender shoot, a root, a scrawny seedling, a scrubby plant. He is not beautiful to look at, like treasure, nor physically awesome like a ship, and he isn't the tallest tree, like Caiaphas the Great High Priest, or Pilate, the Roman Governor, and all the other political heavyweights who decide Jesus' fate. He is an ordinary-looking man, possibly even ugly, who rides into Jerusalem on an ass and dies a shameful death on two bits of wood. He's no film star, no bionic stuntman, no church bigwig. But this tender shoot has the most tender heart in history; he came down to earth to die a horrible death, motivated by pure love for each and every one of us.

A few weeks back I went on a woodland walk with my boys. We started off near some wilderness, then a clear path emerged. We followed it for a while, then stopped for a picnic on a big pile of chopped logs. On the hill in the distance you could see rows and rows of tender saplings, their spindly trunks protected by plastic tubes. It served as a metaphor to me of Lent, or at least how Lent can be for many of us. A time of wilderness, a time of brokenness, a time of being chopped down to size, but then also a time of emerging pathways, of renewal and rebirth as we head towards the resurrection.

Perhaps sometimes, to return to my opening thoughts, we can lay a little too much store by being a tall tree. I know that I can take a little too much pride in my sense of personal identity rather than in Christ himself. Sometimes we can lose that sense of who we are actually meant to be – containers for Christ. I think I was meant to see that pile of logs in the forest. Like the beams in our story, until we are willing to be chopped down, to die to ourselves as Christ did on the cross, and accept being no more than a tender shoot, a spindly sapling, then we have not grasped the message of the cross. For his strength is made perfect in our weakness. Sometimes we put ourselves on pedestals; sometimes we put others on pedestals, making tall trees of each other. We think we are strong or we elevate others, only to discover we're little more than a community of broken people. There is hope. God loves a scrawny seedling, a tender shoot that he can fill with his strength, Jesus Christ. And I am rather scrawny at the moment, as many of you have noticed!

There was an interesting interview with the Bishop of Bradford, Nick Baines, in the *Radio Times* this week. He was speaking about the much-covered Leonard Cohen song, 'Hallelujah'. The song speaks of the 'holy and the broken hallelujah' – Baines says that this is 'a phrase that encapsulates the torn nature of human beings who long to be "holy", but usually manage just to be "broken". Cohen's point is that God is not surprised by this'. I speak to you today as someone who longs to be holy, but more often than not ends up broken. I never really considered until the last few weeks that that might just be part of God's plan.

Before we move into a time of prayer, I leave you with three questions to ask yourself:

Do I long to be beautiful?
Do I long to be strong?
Do I long to be holy?

The solution to all three questions is found at the cross, when we crucify the self and hold Jesus within. He alone makes us beautiful, strong and holy ... we cannot do it ourselves.